SCARFACE AL AND THE CRIME CRUSADERS

Chicago's Private War Against Capone

Dennis E. Hoffman

Southern Illinois University Press

Carbondale and Edwardsville

Copyright © 1993
by the Board of Trustees,
  Southern Illinois University
All rights reserved
Printed in the United States of America

Designed by Edward D. King
Production supervised by Hillside Studio

96 95 94 93   4 3 2 1

The paper used in this publication meets the
minimum requirements of American National
Standard for Information Sciences—Permanence
of Paper for Printed Library Materials, ANSI
Z39.48-1984.

Library of Congress
Cataloging-in-Publication Data

Hoffman, Dennis E.
  Scarface Al and the crime crusaders:
Chicago's private war against Capone / Dennis
E. Hoffman.
    p. cm.
  Includes index.
    1. Organized crime—Illinois—Chicago—
Prevention—Case studies. 2. Crime prevention—
Illinois—Chicago—Citizen participation—Case
studies. 3. Capone, Al, 1899–1947. I. Title.
HV6452.I3C36   1993
364.4'3'0977311—dc20   93-16865
ISBN 0-8093-1925-X   CIP

To my wife, Colleen

Contents

Illustrations

Preface

In the 1920s, Chicago businessmen were prosperous and deeply involved in the city's civic affairs. Some achieved distinction merely by being rich, while others made their mark through public service. They led lives of genteel conformity and escaped notice on the front pages of the local newspapers—until the advent of a gangster who was to become known as "Scarface Al."

"Scarface Al" Capone's bullet-strewn path to dominion over gang-dom captivated the media's fancy. Headlines screamed out body counts from "unsolved" gang murders almost daily. Crime stories in the *Tribune* and other Chicago newspapers contained more gratuitous violence than today's Clint Eastwood movies.

Chicago businessmen were acutely aware that their city needed to be cleaned up. But given the ineffectual response of local authorities to organized criminal gangs, prospects for such a housecleaning seemed dim.

The coming of Chicago business leaders to the forefront of crime fighting was, in a sense, inevitable. If, indeed, Chicago was to advance toward its goal of being recognized as a center of culture and civilization, then there was no alternative to a bold change. That change consisted of acknowledging Chicago's organized crime problem and rethinking strategies for attacking it. The essential and novel ingredient in the radical refashioning of crime control was the direct involvement of private businessmen in the battle against "Scarface Al" Capone.

Acknowledgments

Many people have aided in writing this book, but I particularly want to acknowledge my indebtedness to Angus Crawford Randolph and Angus M. C. Randolph for lending me Robert Isham Randolph's scrapbooks. Robert Isham Randolph led the shadowy Secret Six, urban vigilantes who hastened Capone's fall.

I thank John Jemilo for granting me access to the voluminous files of the Chicago Crime Commission and for extending his hospitality to me during my research trips to Chicago. I also am grateful to Susan H. Wilson and Ruth Kissell who carefully edited this book. I owe thanks as well to Angela Patton for ably typing the final manuscript.

Finally, for teaching me about love, faith, hope, and courage, this book is dedicated to Colleen Hoffman.

Scarface Al and
the Crime Crusaders

1

The Rest of the Al Capone Story

With one hand on the steering wheel and the other holding a .45-caliber pistol, Colonel Robert Isham Randolph, the leader of a private gangbusting group known as the Secret Six, drove his automobile from his home in Riverside, Illinois, to the Loop in Chicago.[1] It was late at night in February 1931, and Randolph had not arranged for anyone to tail him. He entered the Lexington Hotel and stepped into an iron-grille freight elevator. After going through various doors and passing numerous thugs and gunmen, he was taken to a suite occupied by a man Randolph had vowed to put in prison, Al Capone.

Capone was seated at a desk, with his back to the wall. Randolph noticed slots in the doors and French mirrors covering the slots. A rifle barrel could be thrust through each slot. Randolph found he could peer through these mirrors and see outside, but persons on the outside could not see in. Capone got up from behind the desk and walked over to greet his visitor. The two shook hands.

Capone said, "Hell, Colonel, I'd know you anywhere—you look just like your pictures."

The tall, thin president of one of the largest chambers of commerce in the world grinned and replied, "Hell, Al, I'd never have recognized you—you are much bigger than you appear to be in photographs."

When Randolph flashed Capone his boyish grin, it lit up the colonel's face, making Randolph seem younger than his forty-six years. Randolph's hair receded from a high forehead, a forehead that wrinkled up until it looked like the map of a railroad switchyard. Randolph removed his coat, for he had heard it was impossible to obtain an audience with Capone without being searched. Next, he gave the pistol he was toting to Capone, who placed it on a chair.

1

"May I use your telephone?" Randolph inquired. "You see, your name has been used to frighten women and children for so long that Mrs. Randolph is worried about me; she knows of my visit. I would like to call her and tell her everything is okay."

"Women are like that," said Capone, as he took Randolph to a phone in another room. When Randolph returned, Capone served him a beer and asked, "Colonel, what are you trying to do to me?"

"Put you out of business," Randolph replied.

"Why do you want to do that?"

"We want to clean up Chicago, put a stop to these killings and gang rule here."

"Colonel, I don't understand you," Capone said. "You knock over my breweries, bust up my booze rackets, raid my gambling houses, and tap my telephone wires, but yet you're not a reformer, not a dry. Just what are you after?"

Before Randolph could answer, Capone said, "Listen, Colonel, you're putting me out of business. Even with beer selling at $55 a barrel, we didn't make a nickel last week. You know what will happen if you put me out of business? I have 185 men on my personal payroll, and I pay them from $300 to $400 a week each. They were all ex-convicts and gunmen, but now they are respectable businessmen, just as respectable as the people who buy my stuff and gamble in my places. They know the beer, booze, and gambling rackets—and their old rackets, rackets that sent them to the can. If you put me out of business, I'll turn every one of those 185 respectable ex-convicts loose on Chicago."

"Well, Al, to speak frankly," said Randolph, "we are determined to put you out of business. We are burned up about the reputation you have given Chicago."

"Say, Colonel," Capone said. "I'm burned up about that, too. Chicago's bad reputation is bad for my business. It keeps the tourists out of town. I'll tell you what I'll do; if the Secret Six will lay off my beer, booze, and gambling rackets, I'll police this town for you—I'll clean it up so there won't be a stickup or a murder in Cook County. I'll give you my hand on it."

Randolph refused to cut a deal with the gangster. Instead, he drank another glass of Capone's beer.

Capone asked, "Say, Colonel, what do you think about the mayoral election? Should I come out for Anton Cermak or ride along with the Republicans and 'Big Bill' Thompson?"

"I think you'd better stick with Big Bill," said Randolph.

Then the colonel put on his coat and hat, and Capone returned Randolph's pistol. "So even respectable people carry those things?" Capone asked laughingly. He shook Randolph's hand and said, "No hard feelings?"

"No hard feelings," said Randolph.[2]

Beyond the Eliot Ness Myth

Robert Isham Randolph was one of the crime crusaders, a loosely organized group of businessmen—all unsung heroes—whose courageous actions helped end Al Capone's domination of Chicago. Some were "givers," donating huge sums of money to finance both private and public crime-attack activities. Others were "doers": conducting special prosecutions of gangsters; applying science to solve gangland murders; inventing catchy phrases such as "Public Enemy Number One" to raise awareness of organized crime; and protecting witnesses so they could testify against Capone in his trial for income tax evasion.

Because of the pervasiveness of the Eliot Ness myth, however, few people know about the crime crusaders. The book entitled *The Untouchables* and the television series and motion picture of the same name have fostered the false notion that Eliot Ness and his outfit of incorruptible Prohibition agents singlehandedly brought Al Capone to justice. But Ness's raids on Capone's operations did not, as the media have claimed, put Capone out of business or into jail.

Oscar Fraley, who helped Eliot Ness write *The Untouchables*, claimed in the foreword of the book that Ness and his Prohibition detail from the United States Department of Justice "smashed Capone's alcoholic empire, cut off his almost inconceivable income, ended his ability to pay millions of dollars a year in graft and helped gather the income tax evasion information which sent Capone to a federal prison."[3] While all of this is true, it's only part of the story of the fall of Al Capone.

The Untouchables contains several clues about the rest the story. At the very beginning of the book there is a dramatic scene in which the members of the Secret Six, a special committee of the Chicago Association of Commerce, are holding a meeting in a cigar-smoke-filled room to decide what should be done about Al Capone. These six men, according to Ness and Fraley, "were gambling their lives, unarmed, to accomplish what three thousand police and three hundred prohibition agents had failed to accomplish: the liquidation of a criminal combine."[4] Who were these men? What motivated them to fight such a ruthless killer as Al Capone? How could private citizens, lacking the authority to use deadly force and make arrests, fight organized crime?

After teasing readers with some tidbits about the Secret Six, Ness and Fraley disclosed that the Secret Six, who had connections "all the way up as high as President Hoover," backed the idea of forming a special unit of Prohibition officers and convinced U.S. Attorney George E. Q. Johnson to name Eliot Ness as the head of the unit. There is one more rather opaque reference to Chicago businessmen in *The Untouchables*. Ness and Fraley reviewed the rise of Al Capone to power, noting that Capone's fatal mistake was in not being content with controlling the liquor, beer, vice, and gambling rackets. They suggested that when Capone began encroaching on legitimate businesses, the citizenry became alarmed. To quote Ness and Fraley:

> It was all right when mobsters were merely eliminating themselves but now people realized that the city was no longer safe for decent citizens. This was what aroused the Chicago Association of Commerce, which didn't dare to take open action because nobody was certain who was or wasn't in Capone's pocket, to form the Secret Six.[5]

More leads for pulling together the rest of the story can be found in books by Elmer Irey, John Kobler, and Robert J. Schoenberg. Irey, the former chief of the Enforcement Branch of the U.S. Treasury, told of how a privately financed undercover agent infiltrated the Capone gang.[6] Aside from this interesting tidbit, however, Irey's book raises more questions than it answers.

Who persuaded the federal government to go after Capone in the first place? Who paid for the undercover agent's foray into the underworld? Who paid for the Treasury Department's unofficial witness protection program that safeguarded witnesses prior to Capone's trial?

John Kobler, author of *Capone: The Life and World of Al Capone*, also explored some of the forces responsible for Capone's demise.[7] Kobler's account stressed the importance of a two-pronged attack, the one by

Ness and his Untouchables to wreck Capone financially and the other by the Internal Revenue agents to send Capone to prison. Kobler made passing references to the Chicago Crime Commission's public enemies list, the Secret Six, and Colonel Robert R. McCormick's participation in the investigation of the Jake Lingle murder in 1930. Yet he stopped short of probing into "how" the private sector fought gangsters.

In *Mr. Capone*, Robert J. Schoenberg correctly pointed out that Ness did *not* contribute directly to Capone's "undoing."[8] The government never tried Capone on the only indictment for which the Untouchables gathered evidence—conspiracy to violate the Prohibition laws. Schoenberg alluded to the crime-fighting work of several Chicago businessmen but only scratched the surface in dealing with their role in Capone's fall.

The Rise of Al Capone

Before one can begin to understand why Capone fell from power, it is necessary to review how he rose to become the leader of Chicago's underworld. Born in Brooklyn, New York, on January 17, 1899, Capone lived the rowdy life of a lad hanging on the fringe of the Five Points gang, which had been involved in criminal violence for almost a century. In his late teens, Capone drew the attention of Johnny Torrio, then a power in the Five Points gang. After Torrio moved to Chicago to aid the underworld enterprises of James ("Big Jim") Colosimo, Torrio sent for Capone in 1919.

Capone was already marked by the signs of violence that gave him a nickname distasteful to him. Two ugly, jagged scars—tokens of his career as bouncer in the Harvard Inn, a brothel-saloon in Brooklyn— plowed his left cheek. Because of those scars, newspaper reporters pinned the epithet "Scarface Al" on him. Capone grew more bitter every time the press used this nickname in referring to him. Not even Capone's closest henchmen dared use it.

When Capone joined Torrio in Chicago, bootlegging was an undeveloped undertaking. Johnny Torrio, a soft-spoken, retiring person, served as foreman of Colosimo's gambling and prostitution dives along 22nd Street in Chicago. Torrio's recruit naturally went into the business. Capone established the Four Deuces, so named because of its address, 2222 South Wabash Avenue, and it prospered despite a lack of elegance. Capone also managed Jim Colosimo's Cafe, a famous restaurant featuring great entertainers such as jazz singer Al Jolson and Isham Jones's Ragtime Band. When Colosimo met death from a gun in 1921, Torrio moved into his place and Capone advanced a notch, still a protégé, but in a key position, for the trade in liquor was expanding.

"Bloody" is the word that best characterizes the early history of Torrio's fight for monopoly over the bootlegging business. The Chicago Sicilians, led by the Genna brothers, rapidly established huge, illegal alky-cooking plants (where denatured alcohol was made fit for drinking) and became the confidants of Mike Merlo, head of the powerful Unione Siciliana, a fraternal benefit insurance society that provided cover for gangster operations. While Merlo lived, peace prevailed. Independent bootlegging gangs split the city into sectors, and all waxed rich.

Then Merlo died a natural death in 1924, upsetting the underworld truce. Suddenly every gangster in Chicago wanted control of the Unione, which sold death benefit insurance to all immigrants from Italy and Sicily. Whoever owned the society possessed a treasury as great as any to be found among labor unions.[9] Before Merlo's spectacular funeral cortege paraded the streets of Chicago with a life-sized waxen figure of the dead man in the leading car, the killings began. Dion O'Banion, the north side gang leader, who had resisted invasion of his territory by Capone and Torrio, was slain in his flower shop on November 10, 1924, by three men who he believed had come to buy a floral display for Merlo.

Following O'Banion's assassination, members of his gang suspected the Gennas of murdering their leader, and so they mowed down the Gennas with machine-like precision. Hymie Weiss, O'Banion's successor, and other lesser leaders also fell by the guns. At last only two powerful gangs remained—the Capone gang and the north side gang controlled by "Bugs" Moran, Jack Zuta, and Joe Aiello.

This was 1928 and Torrio had long since fled, frightened by a hail of slugs that had almost killed him in 1925. Capone reigned supreme over his sizable gang inheritance and made underworld history by his conquests of Cicero, Berwyn, Stickney, and other western suburbs. He ruled one of the largest and most sophisticated criminal operations in the history of the United States, estimated to gross between $12,000,000 and $70,000,000 a year. By 1928, "Scarface Al" had become a name known in every American home.[10]

Puppydog or Supervillain?

The basis of Capone's fame and notoriety was a contradiction. As overlord of a vast criminal empire, Capone, more than any other person, was responsible for the rampant lawlessness and massive corruption that plagued Chicago in the twenties. At the same time, Capone's colorful persona captured the imagination of the popular press and the public, transforming him into a mythic folk figure.[11]

The general public admired Capone's defiance of an unwanted law and his flamboyant life-style. His "rags to riches" climb to fame, wealth, and power captivated the public and made him a favorite of the common person on the street. Whenever he appeared in public, people clamored to shake his hand and wish him well. Stories circulated about his generosity, such as giving ten newsboys on the streets twenty-dollar bills and operating a soup kitchen for the poor. Even Capone's automobile achieved legendary status among the public. It was a custom-built, armor-plated Cadillac with bulletproof glass. The appearance of Capone motoring around in his portable fort in downtown Chicago was always an occasion of public interest. "There goes Al," people would say, and pedestrians would crowd to the curb, craning their necks for a glimpse of Capone.

One reporter who interviewed Capone in 1930 found him "intelligent, happy-go-lucky, affable . . . with a dark, kindly face, sparkling eyes . . . harmless as a St. Bernard puppydog."[12] This popular image of Capone depicts him as a chummy, sentimental, philosophical fellow— the kind you'd invite over for Sunday brunch to talk baseball.[13]

In contrast to this sanitized, romantic image that some journalists and the public have fallen in love with, there were the realities of Capone's violent nature and brutality. During Prohibition, a minority of the gang murders in Chicago were committed under the leadership of Johnny Torrio, Capone's mentor and predecessor as overlord of gangdom. The majority were carried out under the leadership of Capone. Unlike Torrio, who invoked violence only as a last resort,

Capone was temperamental and did not hesitate to send his thugs to commit murder and mayhem whenever he thought it was necessary.[14]

From the vantage point of Chicago's business leaders, Capone exacted too heavy a toll in violence and loss of life to be considered "as harmless as a St. Bernard puppydog." In the late twenties, business leaders rallied round the goal of getting Capone, the symbol of all that was hateful about gang rule in their city. To them, Capone was a supervillain—an aggressor whose indisputable nastiness made it easier to comprehend why Chicago often seemed like a dangerous place to live. For pure evil, community leaders ranked Capone up there with Satan.

"The Chicago Problem"

The vilification of Al Capone by Chicago's business elite represented an overpersonalization of the hostile forces in their city. By concentrating their attention on Capone, they overlooked a greater source of trouble—Prohibition.

A mere perusal of the content of the daily newspapers at the onset of Prohibition underscores this point. On the morning of January 16, 1920, the *Chicago Tribune*, then under the control of Colonel Robert R. McCormick, featured this front-page headline: "NEW WAR LOOMS; BRITAIN FEARS DRIVE ON INDIA BY SOVIET VICTORIES OF RUSSIAN REDS BRING CRISIS." Beneath this early indication of anticommunism was a small one-column story headed: "LIQUOR KNELL TO TOLL IN U.S. AT MIDNIGHT; LAST RITES JOYLESS THOUGH LAW NODS." It began:

> General prohibition arrives tonight at the stroke of twelve. Liquor which had most of the robustness knocked out of it on the first of last July takes official leave of its life in the USA tonight. Trucks, limousines, and baby buggies rumbled from saloons, stores, and hotels with liquor stocks. Fifty thousand gallons of booze moved from public places to private homes last week.[15]

It is obvious that Colonel McCormick was more interested in the upheavals in Russia since the most noticeable part of the front page was a photograph of a bearded man captioned: "Nicolai Lenine: Leader of the Russian Bolsheviks whose power threatens the peace of the world."[16] Colonel McCormick misjudged the significance and the problems to his own city with which Prohibition was loaded.

When bootleggers emerged to quench the city's thirst, Al Capone occupied a position no different from that of Chicago's business leaders. Like any entrepreneur, Capone faced the contradictions at the very heart of Chicago life. The main contradiction, "the Chicago problem," was simple: Chicagoans wanted *both* a wide-open city and a good reputation. Upon assuming leadership over Chicago gangdom, Capone may have had little inkling of the "the Chicago problem." Capone was by nature reckless and violent, given to the "grand gesture." His natural flamboyancy might, in normal times, have led him either to being machine-gunned to death or to a peaceful retirement in Florida where he owned a luxurious mansion.

By the late twenties, however, Chicago's tolerance for publicity-seeking murderers had run out. Something had to be done. The choice facing community leaders had already become clear during the planning meetings for the 1933 Chicago World's Fair. That choice was between a wide-open city whose national and international reputation would slide even further into the gutter and a city that ridded itself of the sinister strongman responsible for Chicago's shameful reputation.

2

Who Were the Crime Crusaders?

The two Chicagos that the world knew during the twenties—the political Chicago and the chamber of commerce Chicago—featured few men with the stature, integrity, and intestinal fortitude to stand up to Al Capone. Political Chicago was a stage for buffoonery, mountebanking, and the sharing of spoils, with mediocrity entrenched in its offices, and waste and corruption everywhere. The condition was changeable, but voters were too apathetic to take action. Reformers constantly complained of "slacker citizenship" at the polls.

By contrast the chamber of commerce Chicago was typified by the finespun phrases and platitudes of the after-dinner speaker. It could be characterized by the railroad executive who sat in on President Hoover's prosperity conference, following the collapse of the stock market in the fall of 1929, chimed in on the yeah-man chorus on 1930 expansion programs to avert unemployment, and returned to lay off 1,500 shopmen. The chamber of commerce Chicago supplied men for citizens' advisory boards and committees but few for practical duty in the trenches of crime fighting.[1]

As a general rule, both politicians and businessmen in Chicago feared Capone and did not dare to oppose the gang leader. Charles G. Dawes, Frank J. Loesch, Burt A. Massee, Calvin Goddard, Colonel Robert R. McCormick, Henry Barrett Chamberlin, and Robert Isham Randolph were exceptions to the rule. The backgrounds, patterns of life, interests, and politics of these men were similar. They were generally well educated, widely traveled, and had access to political and financial resources. All were prominent in their respective businesses or professions. And there were no cowards among them.

Charles G. Dawes

While Al Capone is Chicago's "best-known" citizen, Charles G. Dawes was arguably Chicago's "best" citizen. Banker, comptroller of the currency under President McKinley, vice president under President Coolidge, ambassador to Great Britain, chairman of the Reconstruction Finance Corporation—Dawes was all of these and more. Despite his affluence and political clout, he was preoccupied with serving his city and his country and less concerned with money, power, and status. He lived in suburban Evanston, but he knew the importance of Chicago to the nation. His urge to create a better Chicago led him to find a way to get the federal government involved in his city's battle against Prohibition-era gangsters.

In a sense, the life of Charles Dawes was an extension of the lives of his ancestors. William Dawes, the great-great-grandfather of Charles Dawes, rode with Paul Revere on the night of April 18, 1775. Revere took the route from Charlestown to Lexington; Dawes ducked the redcoats through meadows and marshes from Boston to Concord. Another great-great-grandfather of Charles Dawes was Manasseh Cutler, a graduate of Yale before the Revolutionary War and a friend of Benjamin Franklin. Cutler helped draft the Ordinance of 1787, the charter for the government of the Northwest Territory. The most important provision of the ordinance was the abolition of involuntary servitude—the first effective blow struck against slavery in the United States. Rufus R. Dawes, of the third Dawes generation in Ohio, came out of the Civil War a brevet brigadier general. Charles Gates was the son of Rufus R., who owned the Marietta Iron Works, manufacturers of railroad iron.[2]

Charles Dawes grew up in Marietta, Ohio, where he attended Marietta College and received both bachelor of arts and master of arts degrees. Working as an engineer on a small Ohio railroad, he earned sufficient money to put himself through Cincinnati Law School, from which he graduated with a bachelor of laws degree. He taught himself music, first mastering the flute and then the piano. His composition "Melody in Minor" was played by distinguished artists throughout the world. Admitted to the bar in 1886, he practiced law in Lincoln, Nebraska, before moving to Evanston, Illinois, in 1894. Dawes organized the Central Trust Company of Illinois in 1902 and was president until 1921; chairman of the board from 1921 to 1925; honorary chairman of the board in 1930–1931.[3]

After being commissioned major of engineers of the National Army in 1917, Dawes was promoted to brigadier general and awarded the Distinguished Service Medal. Dawes served as purchasing agent for the American Expeditionary Forces under the command of General John J. Pershing.

Following World War I, Dawes formed in 1923 the Minute Men of the Constitution. The context in which the Minute Men emerged featured the corrupt crowd of Chicago Mayor William Hale ("Big Bill") Thompson controlling city government, Governor Len Small's shady cohorts running state government, the Ku Klux Klan ascending to power in downstate Illinois, and labor hoodlums making building operations in the nation's second largest city as dangerous as a battlefield. Dawes opposed Thompson, Small, and the KKK, but was not anti-union. In starting the Minute Men to assist law enforcement, Dawes said: "This country needs a new Bill of Rights, just as it did when the Declaration of Independence was signed. We need to protect the country from those who are trying to dig under the cornerstone of the Constitution. Our organization is not a political body, but we are going to fight for clean politics."[4]

The Minute Men's first test came in Cook County in a judicial election. Labor bosses attacked two respected judges, Denis E. Sullivan, a Democrat, and Jesse E. Holdom, a Republican, as "injunction judges." Dawes rallied his two companies of Minute Men behind the judges. Minute Men rang doorbells and manned the polls on election day. Heavy majorities for Sullivan and Holdom in the suburbs, running nine to one in Evanston and almost as much in others, carried the day. Dawes saw the election of these two judges as representing victories over gangsters who had seized control of labor unions in Chicago.

Called again to serve his country in 1924, Dawes accepted the nomination of the Republican Party to run for vice president on the same ticket with Calvin Coolidge."[5] American voters elected Calvin Coolidge president and Dawes vice president of the United States in November 1924. During his vice presidency, Dawes was finance chairman and his brother, Rufus C. Dawes, president of A Century of Progress Exposition, Chicago's World's Fair. Conceived during the

1920s, the exposition was pushed through to completion despite the Depression of the 1930s. Chicago and the Dawes brothers organized an exposition that drew more visitors than any previous world's fair.[6]

Frank J. Loesch

Frank J. Loesch's career reached back to the days of Julius Grinnell, Judge Gary, and Joseph Medill (the nemeses of the 1886 anarchists), and other fighters for Chicago's welfare. The Great Fire, the Pullman strike, the political upheavals and social crises—he knew all these as an eyewitness and as a participant. He had been a school trustee and a special prosecutor of election frauds but had never held elective office. Working as a bookkeeper for a telegraph company, he had "studied law nights at Union Law School (now Northwestern Law School)," and while in his middle thirties, he had become a reputable Chicago attorney.[7]

Perhaps, there was a reason, in the late twenties, for his still looking the part of a fighter: his mother's father had been one of Napoleon's soldiers, and his father had served in the army of the grand duke of Baden. Of various tasks that fell to him such as the leadership of the Chicago Bar Association, the one to which he was elected early in 1928 proved to be that which returned him to the political battlefield. It was the presidency of the Chicago Crime Commission, whose extensive records and reports were unsurpassed, but whose effectiveness in combatting organized crime stopped at that point.[8]

In taking over the leadership of the Commission, Loesch practically deserted a lucrative law practice, one that numbered among its clients some of the nation's largest institutions, so that he could devote his time to battling Al Capone. In the minds of most of Loesch's contemporaries, any businessman who would do that must be one of three things: a crazy man, a crank reformer, or a publicity seeker.

Loesch's fellow businessmen wondered what inspired him to forsake the mahogany conference rooms of large corporations to lead a movement directed at gangsters toting Thompson machine guns. Delving into his writings and into his past offers several answers.

For one thing, the moral imperatives of Christianity motivated Loesch. For twenty-five years, he served as an elder of the Fourth Presbyterian Church of Chicago, where he taught a Bible class every

Sunday morning.[9] Loesch believed that only through a "Christian approach" to public service could the ideals of Jesus Christ be brought to bear upon the destruction of the sources of evil in the world. As a Christian, Loesch felt a duty to provide unselfish, direct assistance to anyone suffering or in dire need. This principle called "Samaritanism" is associated with the New Testament story of the Good Samaritan, the traveler who stopped to give aid to an injured stranger. Samaritanism created in Loesch an obligation to help those in need—regardless of whether the needy was a lone individual or an entire city.[10]

Loesch's motivation for pursuing the cause of crime fighting also derived from his love for Chicago. A spark of pride and devotion to the city was kindled in him during two gruesome nights in October 1871, when as a lad of nineteen and a stranger in Chicago, he scurried about the burning metropolis helping a frantic mother and her young ones; tearing up fences with hands that were lacerated; and plowing up a field that in the morning was revealed as a refuge spot for 3,000 people. The backbone of the man is revealed in the following excerpt from his own little book of memoirs of the Great Fire:

> The South Side was a mass of smoking ruins. . . . After some difficulty, I found only a few square feet of unbroken stone, and a warm stone at that, upon which I could sit amongst the ruins of my former business place and observe what was going on. I was there about an hour meditating on what course to pursue and what city I could go to. I had only two dollars in my pocket and had the impression that Chicago would, of course, disappear as a business place. Then, I saw a score of men at work in the ruins of the Chamber of Commerce at the corner of Washington and La Salle Streets. They were actually removing debris, smoking hot, preparatory to rebuilding. . . . I walked alone down South Clark Street to about Twelfth Street where I observed an apple pie in a baker's window. Fearing the price would put a big dent in my two dollars, I entered with some timidity to inquire. To my surprise, it was only twenty cents which I joyfully paid. My courage rose to the point of asking permission to eat the pie in the shop. This being granted, I disposed of the pie, which was delicious, and left the shop with my morale boosted to the sky. I walked on with the most intense feeling of pride that Chicago would come back and I must stay right here.[11]

Chicago patriotism thrust Frank Loesch into the presidency of the Crime Commission in 1928, and his Christian faith sustained him for the next three years in a relentless quest to rid his city of political corruption and criminal gangs. Loesch, like other reformers, regarded Chicago as a city in chains—a place whose city hall and county building had cast across them the shadow of Al Capone.

Burt A. Massee and Calvin Goddard

Burt A. Massee, Chicago business executive, served as foreman of the coroner's jury that investigated the St. Valentine's Day Massacre. Massee spent part of his business life with the Palmolive company, builder of the skyscraper later known as the Playboy Building, 900 N. Michigan Avenue. He was executive vice president and a director of the Colgate-Palmolive-Peet Company through the twenties. Massee's wife, Kate Webber Massee, was the former club editor of the *Chicago Tribune* and onetime writer of the "Front Views and Profiles" column in that newspaper. She worked for the *Tribune* from 1918 to 1929.

As head of the coroner's jury that investigated the gangland slaying of seven men in a north side garage on February 14, 1929, Massee recommended formation of the first independent crime laboratory in the United States. It came into existence in 1930.

Massee's leadership in developing the crime lab typified the sort of avant-garde niche that he occupied in Chicago. As a member of Chicago's exclusive Skeeters Club, Massee strove to keep a step ahead of the average citizen in knowing what was in vogue in the arts and sciences. The Skeeters met for conversation and friendship on Saturdays at noon in the presidential suite of the Hotel LaSalle. "No women and no free trips" (every member paid his own travel expenses on club trips to Europe and other faraway places)—those were the rules. Carl Sandburg sometimes dropped in to read his latest poems, and scientists came by to discuss their most recent discoveries.[12]

The prospect of founding the nation's first scientific crime lab probably seemed like another adventure into unexplored territory for Massee. A devotee of geographical science, Massee was a fellow of the Royal Geographical Society of London and financed an expedition to the Mountains of the Moon in British East Africa in 1928. He once owned one of the largest yachts on the Great Lakes, the *Margo*.[13] The soft-spoken, Harvard-educated Massee often took the scientists who worked at the crime lab for trips on his yacht.

Calvin Goddard, the director of the lab, accompanied Massee on several yachting excursions on Lake Michigan. A renowned firearms expert, Goddard's credentials reveal his diverse background: M.D. degree from Johns Hopkins University, 1915; physician at Johns Hopkins Hospital, 1923–1924; officer in the Medical Corps of the U.S. Army, 1925–1928; and partner in the Bureau of Forensic Ballistics (a private ballistics consulting firm in New York), 1928–1929.

As an army officer, Goddard became familiar with weaponry, visited all the factories of private manufacturers of arms in the United States, and studied their bullets and weapons. Goddard refined his knowledge of ballistics while working at the Bureau of Forensic Ballistics with Charles E. Waite, who had established a system of bullet and firearm identification similar to the Bertillon system of fingerprint identification.[14] Goddard and Waite developed a number of items of equipment for examining firearms evidence, the most important of which was the adaption of the comparison microscope for the comparison of bullets and cartridge cases.[15] Goddard and Waite were credited with the discovery that each rifle barrel imparted unique markings on bullets. This ability to establish that a bullet had been fired from a particular weapon was proclaimed the "new science of forensic ballistics."

The most important test of Goddard's comparison microscope prior to his work in the crime lab in Chicago came in 1927 when he served as an expert witness in the Sacco-Vanzetti case. Conflicting testimony of prosecution and defense gun experts marked the trial of Sacco and Vanzetti for murders committed during the course of a payroll robbery in 1920. After appeals for a retrial had failed, Goddard volunteered to reexamine the evidence with his comparison microscope during the course of a review for the governor of Massachusetts. Goddard's results agreed with those of the prosecution's witnesses. The defendants were subsequently executed.[16]

Robert R. McCormick

Colonel Robert R. McCormick owned the *Chicago Tribune* during the twenties, but what most people today remember about him is his Tribune Tower, which was built in 1925. Thirty-six stories high, McCormick's creation remains one of the most distinctive office buildings in Chicago. To the medieval sculptural ornamentation of the exterior, McCormick added souvenir fragments—bricks and stones from famous buildings and sites all over the world such as the Great Pyramid, Notre-Dame de Paris, the Great Wall of China, and St. Peter's Basilica. This element in McCormick's taste was balanced by American fragments such as a brick from Independence Hall, a piece from the Alamo, and a rock from Mark Twain's "Injun Joe" cave.[17]

The colonel was the fifth Robert McCormick in his family's American history. The first, a son of an Ulster immigrant to Pennsylvania, fought in the Revolutionary War under Nathanael Greene and helped bottle up Cornwallis in Yorktown. During the war, the family moved to the Shenandoah Valley of Virginia where a second Robert was born. Robert McCormick II, a tinkerer, tried to build a mechanical reaper. His son Robert III died of the "flux," but another son, Cyrus, took over the reaper and made it work.

Moving to Chicago in 1847, Cyrus McCormick created a manufacturing and sales empire. As a transplanted southerner, Cyrus McCormick sympathized with the South over the slave controversy. Joseph Medill, the editor of the *Tribune*, labeled Cyrus McCormick "poor white trash" and a "man-stealer." Yet history records that Joseph Medill's daughter Katherine married Cyrus's nephew Robert Sanderson McCormick. From this unexpected alliance came Robert Rutherford McCormick, born on July 30, 1880.[18]

Robert R. McCormick graduated from Yale University in 1903, studied law at Northwestern University, and gained admission to the Illinois Bar. He entered politics in 1904 when he was elected alderman from the old Twenty-first Ward. In 1910 he was called on to assume the presidency of the Tribune Company.[19] In his time, McCormick was dubbed a "nonconformist" and a Chicago "patriot." Even though he was a conservative Republican, he fought battles against two great Chicago Republicans, Boss William Lorimer and "Big Bill" Thompson. The most Republican of presidents, Herbert Hoover, failed to please McCormick.

Throughout the twenties, McCormick advocated the repeal of Prohibition. But for a single event, however, the colonel would never have joined the other crime crusaders in their war against Al Capone. That event was the murder of *Tribune* reporter Alfred "Jake" Lingle in 1930. Not the kind of man who "would turn the other cheek," the

Colonel sought to avenge the gangland assassination of one of his own employees.

Henry Barrett Chamberlin

No one in Chicago—not even Colonel McCormick—was better suited to the task of using publicity to checkmate Al Capone than Henry Barrett Chamberlin. Serious-minded Chicagoans for three decades associated his name with newspaper and publicity work, as an investigator of social and civic conditions, as a writer of news stories, and as a leader in crime-fighting reform. Many who knew him only as a newspaper man and as the director of the Crime Commission did not realize that he was a lawyer by profession, who had taken his law degree at the Union College of Law.

Prior to becoming director of the Crime Commission, Chamberlin had been a police reporter and had risen to become editor of the *Chicago Record Herald*. He also edited several magazines, including *Chamberlin's Magazine*. He knew Chicago and its political needs because he had served as executive director of the Municipal Voters League. The League was associated with 500 of Chicago's leading business and professional men, all devoted to the best interests of the city. From his work with the League, Chamberlin saw how expensive it could be for the citizenry when voting was neglected and unworthy men slipped into office. The League's goal was the elimination from the Chicago City Council of grafters—called "gray wolves"—and the election of honest men as aldermen.

A spectacular daytime robbery of the Winslow Brothers iron plant in Chicago on August 28, 1917, convinced Chamberlin that something had to be done to stop crimes of violence. In the Winslow Brothers robbery case, "Ammunition Eddie" Wheed and three others stole the payroll money at the iron plant, killed two Brinks Express guards, and stood off 250 police for two hours in a siege at Wheed's mother's house. This was before the days of the tear gas bomb, and police were about to dynamite the house when Wheed surrendered. This crime stirred the city, causing Chamberlin to appeal to the Chicago Association of Commerce to launch and finance the Crime Commission.

"Crime is a business," Chamberlin said, in promoting the new organization to combat lawlessness. "It is an organized business and it must be fought with business methods."[20]

After the Association of Commerce established the Chicago Crime Commission as an independent, nonpolitical, and unofficial agency in 1919, it hired Chamberlin as the Commission's first operating director. Speaking before the annual meeting of the American Institute of Criminal Law and Criminology in Indianapolis, Indiana, on September 17, 1920, Chamberlin explained the Commission's goals: "The Commission is not a vigilance organization for the purpose of apprehending offenders. It is a business organization that helps criminal justice officials to secure the necessary tools to work with. In addition, it monitors agencies charged with the law enforcement."[21]

The Commission became the leading exponent of the speedy trial, sure conviction, and severe punishment. Chamberlin, who served as operating director from 1919 to 1941, firmly believed in the classical school of criminology with regard to criminals, maintaining that "the man or woman who believes that the existing criminal class can be tolerated, and that eighty percent can be converted into useful citizens is a dreamer with faith in and hope for the utterly impossible."[22] Chamberlin held that the punishment of the individual murderer, gunman, or bandit "is necessary as a crime deterrent."[23] Consistent with his belief in punishment, Chamberlin subscribed to the notion of free will. "Deprivation and want cause few crimes in Chicago," he said. "Chicago criminals are criminals by choice—they participate in unlawful enterprises because it's profitable to do so."[24]

As operating director of the Commission, Chamberlin supervised a small staff of court observers, investigators, and record keepers. He acted as unofficial adviser to administrators of criminal justice agencies in Chicago and Cook County and edited the Commission's journal *Criminal Justice*. At first Chamberlin had one "observer" stationed at the criminal court building, and later he had one in each courtroom. In those postwar days the criminal court was a volcano of action, starting with the "Black Sox" baseball scandal that produced indictments and trials. Chamberlin worked with his friend Charles C. Fitzmorris, chief of police, who had been a newspaper reporter himself in his younger days. Chamberlin also established close ties between the Commission and the Cook County state's attorney's office.

Almost immediately after Chamberlin took over as director, he discovered that there were no adequate criminal records in Chicago. Starting with January 1, 1919, the staff of the Commission indexed every burglary and robbery reported in the city and all homicides in the county. By examining the Commission's records, Chamberlin could discover at which stage in the processing of a criminal case that police work or prosecution had broken down. Such information formed the basis of the Commission's numerous statistical reports on crime in Chicago. It also made it easier for Chamberlin to approach criminal justice authorities and the press, since both were interested in accurate, detailed, and pertinent facts on crime.

To foster changes in criminal justice in Chicago, Chamberlin manipulated the press. His years of experience as a reporter and editor enabled him to frame issues in a way that attracted the press's attention. His experience as a journalist gave him a sense of timing, a facility in marshaling facts and presenting arguments in terms that reporters could easily grasp, and a sense for what editors considered newsworthy. Having the newspapers on his side and knowing how to get results through publicity proved essential in 1930 when Chamberlin led a crime drive against Al Capone and Chicago's other leading gangsters.

Robert Isham Randolph

Responsibility for the operations of the Secret Six—a group of businessmen whose self-assigned mission was to drive Al Capone out of business and out of Chicago—fell into the capable hands of Robert Isham Randolph, a shoot-straight, act-straight crusader, who served as president of the Association of Commerce. Born in Chicago on April 14, 1883, to Isham and Mary Randolph, he was a descendant of William Randolph, who emigrated from England in 1643 and settled in Virginia near the James River. Robert's father, Isham, was an eminent American civil engineer, who, after serving throughout the Civil War in the Confederate Army, became chief engineer of the Illinois Central Railroad and designed the lock system for the Panama Canal.[25]

The son, Robert Isham, was not a precocious child, and except for an inclination to play pranks, the first fifteen years of his life were uneventful. His parents packed him away to Virginia Military Academy to instill discipline. He graduated from the engineering school of

Cornell University in 1904. From then on the destiny of the man was to be glazed with the extraordinary.

From 1903 to 1907 he waded through muck and mire in his hip boots when the Chicago Sanitary District needed engineers. During this time, he constructed a hydroelectric power plant at Lockport, Illinois; surveyed for the widening and deepening of the Chicago River; and built the bascule bridges across the Chicago River at 22nd Street. After leaving the Sanitary District, he commanded troops in the tropic heat of Mexico and the hellholes of France when war needed men who could lead. Following World War I, he became senior partner in the engineering firm of Randolph and Perkins and was elected president of the Association of Commerce. Independent-minded and strong-willed, Randolph scorned machine politicians and distanced himself from reformers.

With the naming of Randolph to lead the Secret Six, Al Capone faced a new enemy, a foe who went into action in the same manner in which he had led his troops in Mexico and France—without any bands playing. As leader of the Secret Six, his putting a fist into the dike of Chicago's crime situation in 1930 was born of a conviction that Chicago was not a cradle of hoodlums but the center of a vital civilization, that Chicago could be purged, that Chicago could answer the challenge of any city under the sun in greatness.

Yet it took more than mere civic pride to translate Randolph's conviction into action. It took vision and patience. Being a modest man, he did not seek any rah-rah from the people. His aspirations in fighting against Capone and other gangsters were tall business— taller, perhaps, than any Chicago skyscraper. He sought to fashion the Chicago mind to a newer and more lasting sense of duty, impelling the civic mind to a creed of brighter destiny—Chicago could be great if it got rid of the gangs.

Vigilantes or Good Citizens?

The crime crusaders had roots deep in American history. Not only were some of its leaders Americans of old stock, like Charles G. Dawes and Robert Isham Randolph, but their stand against Capone came from a long American tradition of vigilantism. In the late 1920s the crime crusaders spoke and acted for those who were too paralyzed by fear of Capone to do anything. As a group, they represented the interests of all Chicagoans. They sprang into action to fill a vacuum. Finding a total breakdown of criminal justice in their city, they filled the gap.

The early West supplies numerous examples that fit a similar scenario: private citizens setting out to do what sheriffs, police, judges, and other legal officials would not do or could not be counted on to do. Sometimes the vigilantes of the old West justified the taking of matters into their own hands by stating that public officials were too weak; sometimes they claimed officials were corrupt. Vigilantes have always preferred beyond-the-law action because it is quicker, simpler, and less snarled in technicalities.

Even though the crime crusaders displayed the identifying characteristic of vigilantes—group action in lieu of regular justice—they denied being vigilantes. When accused of vigilantism, they would vehemently try to distance themselves from organized, extralegal movements seeking to restore law and order. They preferred to think of themselves as "good citizens" who had been "provoked" by Capone and his gang into taking rightful actions to defend their community. The trouble in the Chicago of the twenties, as the crime crusaders saw it, was long-continued citizen apathy and treasonable public carelessness. Those conditions had brought matters to such an impasse that it was necessary for the "decent element" of Chicago to resort to direct action.

Tracing the situation of gang killings and rampant lawlessness in Chicago to the alliance between criminals and corrupt politicians, the crime crusaders defined the problem of organized crime in terms of a breakdown of citizenship. They held that alliances between criminals and politicians could not exist if the majority of law-abiding citizens made their power felt at the polls in electing honest politicians. From their perspective, civic indifference was at the root of the organized crime problem.

Although none of the crime crusaders set down precise definitions of what they meant by "good citizenship," it is clear from their writings and speeches that their version of citizenship emphasized patriotism and loyalty to Chicago. The term *citizenship*, as they used it, also referred to the capacity for influencing public policy; it implied active involvement in civic and political life. To put good citizenship into practice, the crime crusaders urged their fellow businessmen and professionals to attack organized crime by doing three things: (1) voting in every primary and general election; (2) participating in efforts to arouse public opinion against organized crime and political corruption; and (3) supporting private agencies willing to assist public officers in enforcing the law.

In their own time, the press and the public regarded the crime crusaders as exemplifying good citizenship. They were heroes because they accepted the challenge of defending Chicago against a supervillain who seemed invincible.

3

Why the Feds Stepped In

After Herbert Hoover defeated Al Smith in the presidential election of 1928, he visited Miami as the guest of the chain store magnate J. C. Penney. The Penney estate on Belle Isle was not far from Palm Island, the site of Capone's Florida villa, a fact that gave rise to a myth. According to this fiction, sounds of partying at night from Capone's place, of shooting, shouting, and women screaming, disturbed Hoover's sleep, and he vowed to crush Capone. According to another myth, Hoover got upset because newsmen paid more attention to Capone than to him, on one occasion abandoning Hoover in a Miami hotel lobby so they could interview the gang chieftain.[1]

The truth is that Charles G. Dawes convinced the federal government to step in to tackle Chicago's organized crime problem. President Calvin Coolidge (not Hoover) authorized federal intervention in response to pleas from Dawes, a Chicago banker, who was then Coolidge's vice president.

Petitioning the Senate

Vice President Dawes addressed the U.S. Senate in Washington on behalf of his city's Better Government Association (BGA) on February 27, 1926. Claiming to speak for 200,000 of Chicago's 2,800,000 citizens, Dawes presented an appeal from the BGA to the Senate demanding a federal investigation of outlawry in the area. Dawes painted a panorama of gunmen's funerals attended by public officials; underworld dinners graced by public officers; and of bootleggers, rumrunners, and alien gangsters splitting the profits of murder and thievery with Chicago officeholders. "For the past four years," said Dawes, "there has been growing up in this community a reign of lawlessness and terror, openly defying not only the constitution and laws of the State of Illinois but the Constitution and law of the United States as well."[2]

Dawes used the term "helpless" to describe how Chicagoans felt about combating organized crime. He declared that there had been for a long time in Chicago a colony of unnaturalized persons—blackhanders and members of the Mafia—hostile to the city's institutions and laws, who had formed a supergovernment of their own and who levied tribute upon citizens and enforced collection by terrorizing, kidnapping, and assassinating. There were other gangs, he pointed out, such as the O'Donnells, the McErlanes, Ragen's Colts, and Torrio, some of whom were citizens of the United States. Dawes told the Senate that many of these aliens had become fabulously rich as rumrunners and bootleggers, working in collusion with police and other officials, building up a monopoly in this unlawful business and dividing the territory of the country among themselves under penalty of death to all intruding competitors.

Who was to blame? Dawes assigned responsibility to a secret alliance "between many public officials and underworld assassins, gunmen, rum-runners, bootleggers, thugs, ballot-box stuffers, and repeaters."[3] He charged that a ring of politicians and public officials, operating through criminals and dummy directors, were running five breweries in the city and were selling beer under police protection; that officials, working out of the Chicago Police Department, were convoying alcoholic beverages, namely, whiskey and beer; and that one police officer who was under federal indictment was still acting as a police officer.

As evidence of such a close association between politics and crime, Dawes spoke of particular incidents. He told the senators that Cook County State's Attorney Robert E. Crowe had attended a banquet at the Morrison Hotel in 1924 given by notorious beer lords and booze runners. Dawes also cited the conviction of Cook County Sheriff Peter Hoffman for conspiracy in connection with a jail scandal involving Terry Druggan and Frankie Lake, two Chicago bootleggers. Furthermore, Dawes mentioned the attendance of judges, city and county officials, and politicians as mourners at the funerals of hoodlums slain by gangland's guns.[4]

Dawes hurled his harshest accusations at Crowe. In Dawes's opinion, few officeholders had ever promised so much and delivered so little. Dawes recalled that when Crowe was first elected state's attorney in 1921 with "Big Bill" Thompson's Republican slate, Crowe told the Cook County police, "You bring 'em in and I'll prosecute 'em." As Dawes stated before the Senate, the cases Crowe actually prosecuted were vastly outnumbered by the hundreds of indictments he failed to follow up. During Crowe's first two terms, the number of murders in Cook County almost doubled, an increase Crowe attributed to Prohibition. Of the 349 victims, 215 were gangsters killed in the beer wars. Yet despite the size of Crowe's staff—seventy assistant state's attorneys and fifty police, the largest in the office to that point in Chicago history—it obtained only 128 convictions for murder, none involving gangsters. Bombings during the same period, Dawes pointed out, totaled 369 without a single conviction. While the rise of gangsterism accounted for a good deal of these statistics, it was Dawes's judgment that only gangdom's partnership with police and politicians could explain the low percentage of convictions. There were 2,309 convictions for major crimes of every kind in 1921; in 1923 there were 1,344.[5]

"Not Within Federal Jurisdiction"

Since Dawes charged that most of the criminals involved were aliens, the BGA's petition was referred to the Senate Committee on Immigration, of which Senator Hiram Johnson, Republican of California, was chairman. On March 2, the committee declined to take any action on the BGA's petition on the grounds that it was not within the jurisdiction of the federal government or the Senate to suggest remedies for purely local conditions.[6] It was Senator Johnson's "personal opinion" that:

> every populous American city has its peculiar local problems. Questions relating to vice conditions, corruption, and the thousand and one things incidental to our cosmopolitan character constantly arise.
>
> For a committee of the Senate to undertake investigation of these local problems would be, in the absence of an all-compelling Federal question, a subversion of the fundamental principle of local

self government. An investigation in reference to one great city would invite similar investigations in reference to many. Unless there is something of the most vital consequence to the government and the administration of the Federal laws, it would be, first, an unwarranted interference, and next, a never-ending work for a Senate committee to undertake an investigation of the internal conditions of our great cities.[7]

Chicago Mayor William E. Dever, a Democrat, denied every charge enumerated in the BGA petition. Furthermore, Dever asserted there was no more rum-running in Chicago than in other big cities. As for Dawes's statement that five breweries were operating openly, Mayor Dever said:

> From the investigation I made, I am prepared to brand unreservedly as a falsehood the charge alleged to have been contained in the petition filed by the Better Government Association. I am convinced that both the Federal officials and the city officials charged with responsibility to see that these places obey the law have acted and are acting with honesty and vigor.
>
> Chicago needs no outside help to take care of its crime situation, which, incidentally, I do not believe is any worse than that of any other city of the United States. There is no reason why Chicago's reputation should be bandied about Washington by irresponsible parties.[8]

Whether or not crime conditions in Chicago were as bad as Dawes painted them may have been a debatable point in 1926, but the majority of American newspaper editors, from Seattle to Savannah, agreed that Congress had no jurisdiction over crime in the Windy City. If it had, remarked the *Newark News*, "home rule, local self government, and States' rights would all be junked." "The rest of the country will hardly expect the Government to turn out the Army and Navy for Chicago," caustically observed the *Indianapolis News*. The *Milwaukee Journal* declared that "breaking up an alliance between crime and politics is a local problem." No useful purpose would have been served by meddling in the city's domestic affairs, according to the *Seattle Times*. "What is needed in Chicago," asserted the *Daily News* of that city in a truly prophetic statement, "is an irresistible movement on the part of the citizens, through a strong and fearless judge, a special State's Attorney, and a special grand jury to bring out the facts."[9]

Who Killed McSwiggin?

On April 27, 1926, while Dawes was presiding as president pro tempore over the Senate in Washington, D.C., gangsters were killing William McSwiggin, a young assistant state's attorney, and two other men in Chicago. McSwiggin's slain companions were known gangsters. In the four months prior to McSwiggin's murder, police and newspapers ascribed twenty-nine killings to the booze war—"Gangsters killing gangsters, a good way to get rid of them." But this was an assassination of a public official in the most important office for law enforcement—no longer gangsters killing gangsters, but an attack upon the government. All of Chicago asked, "Who killed McSwiggin?"

Although Dawes spent the greater part of 1926 in Washington, D.C., and played no part in the investigation of the McSwiggin murder, the pitiful performance of local criminal justice officials in the McSwiggin case combined with forthcoming developments in gangland to reinforce in Dawes's mind the necessity of federal intervention. State's Attorney Robert Crowe, who Dawes had singled out in the Senate petition as being corrupt, was the center of attention in the controversial investigation of McSwiggin's murder. Crowe stated that McSwiggin's murder meant "it will be a war to the hilt against gangsters."

Men who knew Chicago politics, however, were skeptical and called for a special grand jury to investigate the murder. Harry Eugene Kelly, then president of the Union League, did not trust the state's attorney. Kelly suggested that an independent fund be raised. He contended that if a grand jury had to depend upon Crowe or the county board for funds, it would be hampered by politics and incapable of free and unbiased action.

Answering this charge through a press release, Crowe claimed that the people of Cook County had elected their state's attorney and did not intend to delegate his powers to "self-appointed investigators." After frustrating the movement for a special investigation and an independent investigator in the McSwiggin case, Crowe summoned a special grand jury, engaged the assistance of Illinois Attorney General Oscar Carlstrom to give the appearance of impartiality, and then presided over the grand jury himself.[10]

By May 5, the newspapers learned that the police had no more actual evidence as to the motives for the shooting and the identity of the killer than they did when it happened. Of the forty-five witnesses who had testified on the day of the murder, none of them would even talk about the McSwiggin murder. On that day, news was released to the *Tribune* that secret warrants had been issued for the arrest of Al Capone, who was suspected of complicity in the murder. According to the *Tribune*, the state's attorney claimed he had established that Capone in person had led the slayers of McSwiggin.[11] Capone, however, proved difficult to find. Raids were made on his haunts. Police arrested his brother John but couldn't locate "Scarface Al." It was later reported that Capone and some of his henchmen were in the woods of northern Michigan, and a squad of police was sent to follow up the tip, but they found no Capone.[12]

Even though the first special grand jury did not discover the murderers of McSwiggin, it managed to unearth a clue. The three victims had been killed by machine-gun fire. Machine guns had only been introduced into gang warfare in Chicago a few months before. If the source of the machine guns could be discovered, possibly the murderers could be traced.

On June 3, Alex Korecek, a hardware dealer, testified before the grand jury that he had sold Thompson machine guns to Charlie Carr, manager of the Four Deuces, which was owned by Capone. Besides this clue, the special grand jury uncovered at every turn the conditions of organized crime in Cook County. Ending the labors of a month, the special grand jury, on June 4, presented a report, which included this explanation of why attacking organized crime was such a difficult task for police and prosecutors: "A conspiracy of silence among gangsters and intimidation of other witnesses after a murder has been committed, immediately operates and there is an element of fear involved because anyone who does aid the public officials by giving facts is very likely to be 'taken for a ride.' "[13]

Public disgust with the work of the first special grand jury served as a threat that civic leaders might push for an inquiry independent of the state's attorney. Upon the expiration of the term of the first grand jury on June 4, Crowe petitioned the chief justice of the criminal court to impanel a second special grand jury. This grand jury went out of existence on July 4, and four more grand juries were impaneled. Under Illinois law, the life of a special grand jury was one month, after which another had to be selected if the investigation was to be continued.

Even though those juries failed to obtain the legal evidence to prove who killed McSwiggin, the case sparked intense public interest in organized crime. It dramatized to the public the alliance between criminal gangs and politics.[14] The failure of the grand juries in solving the mystery of McSwiggin's death demonstrated what Dawes had proclaimed in the BGA's petition: Government in Chicago and Cook County had broken down, and it was helpless when pitted against Al Capone.

Pulling Strings in Washington

Charles Dawes and Al Capone agreed on only one thing—wars between rival gangs over control of the beer market hurt business in Chicago. Capone's profits, like those of "respectable" businessmen depended, in part, on the tourist trade. And if Chicago got a reputation that scared tourists away, everybody would suffer. So Capone sought peace in the underworld. He sent to all surviving gang leaders in the Chicago area an invitation to a peace conference on October 20, 1926, at the Morrison Hotel.[15]

This conference established a bootleg monopoly. Capone dictated the peace pact terms, and the other gang leaders attending the conference accepted them. He partitioned the city up into territories, with each gang responsible for keeping the peace in its own neighborhood. Capone kept the near south side, plus the south and west suburbs.

Each gang would be free to manufacture or import its own beer and liquor or to buy it from whatever source it desired. Within its own territory, a gang could set its own retail prices. The same rules would apply to prostitution and to gambling. No gang would operate handbooks or wirerooms in another gang's territory. No gang would permit any of its pimps to hustle prostitutes in another gang's territory or to put its girls to work in a hotel or rooming house outside its own territory.[16]

Publicity given the 1926 peace conference had repercussions not foreseen by Capone. Chicago's business leaders started for the first time to regard Capone as a significant threat. They began to worry about what the Capone image might be doing to the city's economy. A consensus formed: The time to stop Capone was now.

Charles Dawes and his brother Rufus, who headed the family bank in the Loop, told friends that gang warfare in the Chicago streets was leading some of the men of Wall Street to wonder if their money was safely invested in Chicago. Two decisions were reached. First, the business leaders revived the idea of a world's fair, which had been talked about prior to 1926. Second, they decided that special prosecutors would have to be sent in from Washington to prosecute the city's gangsters.[17]

Concerning the first decision, business leaders felt an exposition larger than anything ever seen before in the Middle West might restore Chicago's reputation. They thought they could bring millions of visitors from every nation and convince the world that Chicago was a safe city. Initially, they estimated it would take ten years to plan and build such an exposition. Since Chicago had been incorporated in 1837, they decided to put on the exposition in 1937 and to call it "A Century of Progress." Before that exposition would open, they planned on having Al Capone behind bars.[18]

The Dawes brothers were important to both decisions. Rufus Dawes became president of the World's Fair Corporation. Charles Dawes recommended as its chief executive an army engineer from Washington, D.C., Major Lenox R. Lohr. When the stock market crashed in 1929, Chicago leaders decided against canceling the exposition. Instead, they moved its opening date up four years. It would open after the next presidential inauguration, in the spring of 1933.

From his office in Washington, Vice President Dawes worked quietly to enlist the federal government's involvement in cleaning up Chicago. A new U.S. attorney was appointed for the Northern District of Illinois in February 1927. He was George E. Q. Johnson. If anybody could withstand the pressures and inducements that Al Capone would employ, it was Johnson. Born on a farm near Ft. Dodge, Iowa, and raised by devoutly religious Swedish parents, Johnson exuded strong moral character. Prior to becoming U.S. attorney, Johnson spent twenty-six years as a lawyer engaged in private practice in Chicago.

Three weeks after Johnson's appointment, the Department of Justice sent to Chicago Dwight H. Green, a young lawyer who had been working in the Washington headquarters of the Internal Revenue Service, or the Bureau of Internal Revenue as it then was called. For nine months Green had labored in the interpretative division of the bureau's legal department, writing opinions on questions involving revenue laws. Then he was transferred to the Board of Tax Appeals Division where he tried cases before the board.[19]

Fate decreed that Johnson and Green would take charge of prosecuting Al Capone and his fellow gangsters. These two would win every case involving a gangster, including the big one against Al Capone in 1931.

When Johnson and Green moved into the U.S. attorney's office in 1928, the prospects for such feats seemed dim. This was Capone's Chicago. Neither Johnson nor Green could have been so clairvoyant as to see their own positioning in the U.S. attorney's office as a harbinger of change in Chicago.

Unleashing the Power of the Federal Government

In the fall of 1928 the man who had greased the wheels of justice in Washington to get honest prosecutors sent to Chicago received a job offer. Frank J. Loesch, president of the Chicago Crime Commission, asked Dawes to lead a movement against the gangsters. Dawes recorded this note in his journal:

> Received a letter from Loesch, the Chairman of the Chicago Crime Commission, asking me in the name of the Commission to undertake the co-ordination of the work of some seven hundred local associations now existing and devoted to constructive civic progress. Loesch and his Crime Commission are in the midst of a crusade against the lawlessness and corruption existing in our city and its government which promises results. The public is at last aroused and the movement, refused support by the City Council, had been financed by popular subscription. It is impossible for me to undertake the work while occupying my present office (of Vice-President), but I have a sincere feeling of regret that I cannot help in the fight upon the lawless element there.[20]

What Dawes wanted most was to get back to Chicago, help the "decent" citizens drive the gangsters out of his beloved city, and assist his brother Rufus in getting the preparations for the Chicago World's Fair under way. Dawes felt, however, that his participation in "direct action" to smash the Capone gang might tarnish the dignity of the office of the vice president. So he did the next best thing to leading the crusade. He lobbied President Coolidge to unleash the power of the federal government against Capone. President Coolidge, acting at the behest of Dawes, authorized the special intelligence unit of the U.S. Bureau of Internal Revenue on October 18, 1928, to begin an investigation of the income tax affairs of Al Capone.[21]

Dawes was destined to play no further role in the crusade because the next president, Herbert Hoover, would draft him to serve as the American ambassador to Great Britain from 1929 to 1932. There were no doubt times during his tour of service in England when Dawes experienced guilt and frustration at not being able to further aid the crusade. But he must have taken solace in the fact that there was at least one other businessman in Chicago who, by virtue of his integrity and grit, was ideally suited to minister to the crime-fighting needs of the city as Dawes was. That man was Frank J. Loesch.

4

Frank J. Loesch and
the Quest for Free Elections

While a citizen of Chicago traveled aboard a steamer returning
from the West Indies in 1928, a radio message came from the Windy
City telling how "Diamond Joe" Esposito had been shot down in the
street. Esposito belonged to the reform faction of the Republican party,
opposing a Capone-backed faction led by Chicago Mayor "Big Bill"
Thompson. Being active in Chicago politics, the citizen knew that
Esposito had been a candidate for ward committeeman in the upcoming primary to be held on April 10. Then another message came
through, reporting the bombing of U.S. Senator Charles Deneen's
home, and still another related how Judge John Swanson's house had
been bombed. Deneen headed the reform faction of the Republican
Party, and Swanson was Deneen's candidate for state's attorney.

After hearing these messages, the Chicagoan knew that "anybody
with red blood in his veins had to show his color and fight against
organized crime and for justice."[1] As quickly as he could get ashore,
he hustled back to the city. His grave voice was heard in many meeting
places. His shrewd but benign face, long-nosed and olive-tinted, his
hair almost white—like the features of an ancient follower of Charle-
magne—was seen on platforms where businessmen gathered to discuss what could be done about Al Capone and underworld crime.

Not everybody knew him. Gallery crowds nudged each other and
asked, "Who's the old guy?" They learned he was Frank J. Loesch.
He was a figure from Chicago's past who, at the age of seventy-six,
had stepped into the violent and troubled scene of Chicago. When
Loesch returned to Chicago from the West Indies, he heard Senator
Deneen speak out: "The criminal element is trying to dominate Chicago by setting up a dictatorship in politics." U.S. Marshal Palmer

Anderson, in a message to U.S. Attorney General Sargent, asked for five hundred deputy marshals to guard the polls on election day. U.S. Senator George W. Norris of Nebraska suggested that President Coolidge withdraw the Marines from Nicaragua and send them to Chicago.[2]

To such an impasse had Chicago come in the spring of 1928. Destructive forces, set in motion through years of paltering with the underworld and tolerating corrupt politicians, had got out of control. So many bombs were tossed by rival political factions during this primary that the press branded it the "Pineapple Primary," in reference to the gangster slang word for bomb.

Primary election day, April 10, was one of sluggings, ballot-box stuffing, kidnapings, and the murder of Octavius C. Granady. Granady was a black attorney and a Deneen opponent of City Collector Morris Eller, a follower of "Big Bill" Thompson, for Republican committeeman of the Twentieth Ward.[3] Not only election workers but voters were beaten, threatened, held hostage, and kept from the polls. Despite all this, Swanson defeated Crowe for the state's attorneyship—a focal point of the campaign in Chicago and Cook County. His margin was 201,227 votes.[4]

In Chicago, the *Herald and Examiner*, a Hearst newspaper, which had championed the Thompson ticket, stated in its leading editorial two days after the election:

> The vote of Chicago in the primaries on Tuesday was a direct and tremendous expression of protest against the lawlessness and violence of booze runners, the gambling managers, the bombmen [sic] and the gunmen of Chicago. The situation had, to the minds of the citizens in general, got past bearing, and they freed their minds in the only way they could—at the polls.[5]

Special Prosecutor

In the aftermath of the Pineapple Primary, something more significant than the defeat of Crowe happened: Loesch was named chief of a staff of special prosecutors and thus became the head of the column marching against Al Capone and Chicago's other gangsters.[6] This occurred because the Chicago Bar Association, through its president, Carl R. Latham, stepped forward to start a fight for free elections in

Chicago. Assisted by Attorney General Carlstrom, the Bar leaders fought through a legal thicket until a special grand jury was appointed to probe election crimes. A special prosecutor was also selected to prosecute crimes committed during the 1928 primary.

The special prosecutor was needed because Robert E. Crowe, the Cook County state's attorney, had a conflict of interest. He could not ethically or effectively prosecute criminal cases such as the Granady murder since the main suspects were members of his own political faction. Then, too, the legal system in Chicago was so shot through with corruption that public confidence required an "outsider" to investigate and prosecute. Latham and other Chicago Bar Association leaders believed the appointment of Loesch, who epitomized honesty and integrity, would instill more confidence in the system.

Despite his reputation as a paragon of virtue, Loesch was not the perfect choice for the job. Whereas ideally the special prosecutor should have been uninvolved in the political complexities attending the crimes that occurred during the primary, Loesch was a partisan. The best choice would have been a specialist in criminal law, yet Loesch's area of expertise was corporate law, and he hadn't handled any criminal cases for forty years. Nevertheless, the Bar Association felt that the benefits of hiring Loesch outweighed the drawbacks.

The scope of Loesch's inquiry included the primary of April 10, 1928, with special reference to the murders of "Diamond Joe" Esposito and Octavius Granady and the bombings of the homes of U.S. Senator Charles S. Deneen and Circuit Court Judge John A. Swanson. Since Attorney General Oscar Carlstrom appointed Loesch, his official title was "Special Assistant Attorney General." Carlstrom also named six members of the Chicago bar as special prosecutors to assist Loesch, including David D. Stansbury, a former assistant U.S. district attorney and a well-known lawyer in private practice.[7]

From the start, Loesch's command of the grand jury investigation was fraught with difficulties. Crowe's friends on the county board blocked an appropriation to finance the investigation, but Loesch said, "I'm ready to fight through this thing without pay for the honor of my profession, Chicago, and Cook County."[8] Citizens raised $150,000 to allow the investigation to go forward. Among the contributors to this private fund were Cyrus H. McCormick, chairman of the board of directors of the International Harvester Company, and William

Wrigley, Jr., owner of the famous chewing gum company and principal owner of the Chicago Cubs.

Because of a plethora of complaints of election crimes and an Illinois law prohibiting any grand jury from being in existence for longer than thirty days, Loesch convened seven special juries to handle the work load. In questioning the veniremen on June 4 for the first grand jury, William V. Brothers, chief justice of the criminal court, asked prospective jurors: "Are any of you connected with any law-enforcing agency?"

F. Edson White, the president of the meat-packing company, Armour and Company, stepped forward and addressed the judge. "I belong to the Chicago Crime Commission. Does that count?" Brothers replied that membership in a private crime-fighting agency such as the Commission did not disqualify anyone.[9]

An important, yet unasked, question was whether or not any of the veniremen held any biases or prejudices against persons associated with the Thompson political organization. If the judge had posed that question, he would have discovered that F. Edson White belonged to the executive committee of the John A. Swanson Business Men's Organization, a reform group whose members were committed to defeating Crowe and the rest of the candidates running on Thompson's ticket. Disregarding any concern about how politics might color a juror's judgment, Brothers picked twenty-three men to constitute the jury and named White as the foreman. In his charge to the jurors, Judge Brothers said:

> Do not hesitate to return an indictment because of the standing, political or social, of any person you believe should be indicted on the evidence presented before you. . . . Be governed only by the law, the evidence presented to you and your convictions. Fear no one. Chicago's fair name—now besmirched by enemies within her own household—must be cleared.[10]

The jury wasted no time, indicting State Senator James B. Leonardo of the Seventeenth District and nine others on June 18.[11] It charged Leonardo with two kidnappings and two assaults to commit murder.

A Great Day for the Fillmore Street Court

The next day five of the gangsters charged by the grand jury were brought before the bench at the Fillmore Street court. Johnny Armondo, one of the five, was held without bail for the murder of Octavius C. Granady. Abe ("Humpy") Klass, Morris Eller's nephew and cousin of Morris's son, Judge Emanuel Eller, was in court, too. He had been freed the night before on a $10,000 property bond approved by Klass's cousin, Judge Eller, after another judge of the municipal court had refused to approve his bail bond. Three others—Sam Pellar, Bennie Zion (alias Yanger), and Joseph Silverman—were held on bonds of $7,000 each on a score of charges of kidnapping and assault to kill, offenses that enlivened the April 10 primary in the Twentieth, Twenty-fifth, and Twenty-seventh wards.

David Stansbury, one of Frank Loesch's aids, wore his customary gray with his silver-knobbed cane, and looked debonair. William H. Haynes, black aid of Loesch's young and serious prosecutors, sat next to Stansbury at the prosecutors' table. A few men and women stepped up before the judge to have their backyard disputes, the ordinary grist of Fillmore Street business, resolved. With those cases disposed of, the bailiff called, "John Armondo, murder; Abe Klass, assault to kill," and so on with the other three.

The door of the bull pen swung open and out came Armondo, just a small fellow, twenty-five years old, rather awed by it all. He came in holding a handkerchief to cover his face and shuffled to the bar. Next was Abe ("Humpy") Klass, Eller's nephew. "Humpy" was a dwarflike creature, with abnormally long arms, an oval-shaped head, smooth black hair, and a sensitive face that twisted in a wry smile as Benny Yanger wisecracked.

Haynes stepped up to tell the court what it was all about. Stansbury stood by his side. Haynes didn't want Armondo admitted to bail. The judge agreed with Haynes and refused to release Armondo on bail. "The others must be held on high bonds," said Haynes.

"How about $10,000 on each count?" asked Stansbury.

"Five thousand," said the defense attorney.

"Ten," said Haynes.

"Let's split it," said the defense attorney. "Make it $7,500 on each count."

The judge set high bonds for three—Zion, $75,000; Pellar, $30,000; and Silverman, $45,000. He ordered Armondo held without bail and freed Klass on a $10,000 bond.

Loesch exuded confidence. In a statement made to the press after the bail hearing, he said, "The killers of Granady are known. We have witnesses who will identify Armondo as one of the men who killed Granady."[12]

Obstructions, Snags, and Hindrances

The obstacles facing Loesch at times seemed insurmountable. When Chicago Police Commissioner Michael Hughes issued an order commanding five of his policemen, who had been rounding up witnesses and indicted persons for the grand jury, to quit assisting the special prosecutor and to return to their regular duties, Loesch subpoenaed the commissioner to testify before the special grand jury on June 26. Loesch threatened to charge Hughes with "obstructing justice," causing the commissioner to rescind his order. Loesch accused Hughes of doing "all in his power to thwart the grand jury's investigations of election crimes."

Vowing he would never again depend on the police "for anything," Loesch laid plans to retain John Stege, a former deputy commissioner of police who had been ousted by the Thompson regime, to carry out law enforcement tasks required by the jury.[13] Stege agreed to take charge of police work in the special grand jury's inquiry, but city and county officials refused to empower him to make arrests. To solve this problem, Loesch asked Cook County Sheriff Charles W. Graydon to deputize Stege. When that didn't work, Loesch tried to convince Police Commissioner Hughes to swear in Stege as a special police officer. Next, he pleaded with Bernard W. Snow, the bailiff of the municipal court, to make Stege a special bailiff. All three efforts failed because of the political fealty Graydon, Hughes, and Snow owed to the Thompson faction of the Republican Party.[14]

David D. Stansbury, Loesch's trusted assistant, and Chief Justice Harry Olson of the municipal court found a way to checkmate city and county officials. They discovered an old law in the Illinois criminal code granting sweeping powers to judges. This law stipulated that judges issuing arrest warrants could authorize private citizens to execute warrants and exercise police powers. The same law stated that judges could require all sheriffs, coroners, constables, and others to aid special agents of the court in the execution of warrants. Chief Justice Olson announced he would issue warrants for all men sought by the special prosecutors and would include in the warrant an order authorizing John Stege to serve it. "That gives Stege the right to bear arms, to make arrests, and to conduct searches for fugitives," said Olson. Ironically, the chief justice's order raised Stege's powers in the special grand jury's investigation above those of some of the officials who had refused to grant Stege any authority.[15]

Defense lawyers for Morris Eller's henchmen made the next move, questioning the legality of the grand jury. Defense attorneys asked Judge Frank Comerford of the criminal court to declare "null and void" all of the special grand jury's indictments. They argued that a special grand jury could not function legally while a regular grand jury was in session and that since a regular grand jury was in session there could be no special grand jury.[16]

Citing a section of Illinois law granting any court the power to order a special venire for a grand jury "at any time when public justice requires it," Comerford upheld Loesch's war on organized crime. The judge said that under the statute the court had the power to summon a special grand jury at any time regardless of whether or not there was another grand jury already in session. "It would be absurd," said Comerford, "to say that in a time of great prevalence of crime when it would be physically impossible for one grand jury to hear all the evidence against all offenders and present them for trial, the court would be powerless to impanel one or more additional grand juries to meet the emergency. Such an inhibition of the powers of the court in such a time would be a travesty of justice."[17]

Undaunted by their failure to have the grand jury declared illegal, Morris Eller's forces took the offensive. Morris's son Judge Emanuel Eller, speaking from the bench of the criminal court where he sat as chief justice while Judge William V. Brothers was on vacation, called the Crime Commission president, Frank Loesch, a "senile fanatic." Judge Eller then ordered a Commission observer to the rear of the courtroom where he could not hear anything, thus denying the observer access to court proceedings.[18]

On July 20 Judge Eller went even further. He used his power as acting chief justice of the criminal court to reduce a bond for one of the men indicted in connection with the murder of Octavius C. Granady. He cut the bond of Sammy Kaplan from $280,000 to $73,000.[19] The next day Judge Eller permitted the release on bonds of two more men who had been indicted for the murder of Granady. In neither case did Judge Eller require the usual investigation of the property schedules for bonds. In one of the cases, he accepted surety that the bond department of the Cook County state's attorney's office had previously rejected because it was overvalued.[20]

Loesch considered Judge Eller's actions "highly improper." In the special prosecutor's view, men upon whose bail Judge Eller had acted belonged to his father's political organization, and the crimes with which the men were charged were part of that organization's political activities. "What, if any, judicial conscience prompted Judge Eller not only to act in proceedings against those working for his father, but to take action in their favor?" asked Loesch. Eller's failure to remove himself because of a conflict of interest, according to Loesch, revealed an "open and brazen use of judicial power to defeat proceedings in the public interest."[21]

When Chief Justice Brothers returned from his vacation, Judge Eller stepped down as acting chief justice. No sooner had this obstacle been removed than Frank Loesch revealed that witnesses called before the special grand jury had been intimidated.[22] One week later, Chicago gangsters shot and killed Bennie Zion, Twentieth Ward gunman, a suspect in the Granady murder case. Zion's murder took place in a west side saloon, a few hours before Morris Eller, boss of the Twentieth Ward, was scheduled to appear before the special grand jury.[23] Zion, a leader of the Eller shock troops in the April tenth primary, had been named in a dozen special grand jury indictments charging beating, kidnapping, and vote stealing. John Stege, chief investigator for the grand jury, said Zion was killed because he had "squawked" to the grand jury. "With Zion out of the way," Stege said, "our case against the Granady killer is in jeopardy."[24]

Commenting on Zion's death, special prosecutor Loesch said: "This goes to show the terror that has gripped the gangsters following the numerous indictments for primary day crimes. Word reached me several days ago that the underworld was terror-stricken and that there probably would be some killings as a result of our efforts."[25]

"We Have Them"

The Loesch-led grand jury indicted City Collector Morris Eller, the boss of the Twentieth ward; his son Judge Emanuel Eller of the supe-

41

rior court; and seventeen of their henchmen for "conspiracy to murder Octavius C. Granady." Among the other charges against the Ellers was that they had swapped police and political protection of liquor, gambling, and vice operators in exchange for votes. When a newspaper reporter characterized the conspiracy indictment as "certainly complete," special prosecutor Loesch grinned. "Gentlemen," he said to a group of reporters, "we have them."[26]

The conspiracy indictment, naming the two Ellers and seventeen of Eller's henchmen, contained twenty-three counts. Among these counts were conspiracy to assault seven different men; conspiracy to murder Granady a few minutes after the polls closed on primary day; conspiracy to kidnap seven men; conspiracy to assault election watchers; conspiracy to prevent by force and intimidation election officials from carrying out their duties; conspiracy to have seven men vote unlawfully; conspiracy to defraud the county by putting persons on the sanitary district payroll for large sums of money to entice them to vote for the Thompson ticket; and conspiracy in giving protection against police interference to persons engaged in bootlegging, gambling, and vice-mongering so they, too, would vote for the Thompson ticket.

Loesch pointed out that the indictments of the Ellers brought to the public's attention the question of whether or not a political boss was legally responsible for criminal acts committed by men working in his interest, under his direction, and in return for substantial rewards. The Ellers protested their innocence, disclaiming all knowledge of the crimes they were indicted for. They demanded an immediate trial, insisting that the special grand jury had indicted them for political reasons. Yet, even the Ellers conceded that in political matters they influenced the men who served them, many of whom had been rewarded by them with well-paying political jobs. Loesch wanted citizens of Chicago as well as the criminal court to consider "what legal responsibility attached to political leadership for the actions of men who were subject to their leaders' guidance and whose political destinies they controlled."[27]

The criminal court addressed Loesch's question on September 18. Defense lawyers for the Ellers made a motion to sever the cases of their clients from the cases against the Ellers's henchmen. Loesch opposed this motion because, if granted, it would force the prosecutors to disclose their evidence in the trial of the Eller henchmen before the principals went to trial. At one point, the arguing between special prosecutor Loesch and defense lawyer Michael Ahern, who would go on to represent Al Capone in the 1931 income tax trial, waxed so hot that the two nearly came to blows. Arguing against splitting the cases of the Ellers apart from the others, Loesch said: "I am no more anxious to be here than you are, your honor. I was forced into the matter just as you have been. I have no more feeling against these defendants, that is, personal feeling, than I have against a piece of wood."[28]

Defense attorneys Ahern and George Guenther leaped to their feet, shouting, "Outrageous! This man has no right to make such a speech here." Ahern yelled, "We want no Messiah talk from a self-righteous Bible thumper here, we want ——"

Loesch turned his back on the judge and faced Ahern. "What do you mean, sir?" he roared.

The two men stepped up to one another, Loesch red with anger, shouting, "What do you mean, sir, what do you mean?"

Ahern continued to yell. "We want no Messiah talk here," he said.

Just as the two men seemed about to throw some punches, Judge O'Connor restored order.

"The interest of public justice," Loesch said, "requires that the Ellers be put on trial with the other defendants. They are trying to escape trial until the funds or the patience of the state are exhausted. Look at the effect on the public if the men higher up are given a change of venue while their tools are put on trial. Two long, expensive trials are put upon the public."

"Irrelevant," said Guenther.

As Guenther was about to continue speaking, Loesch arose from his chair and began to leave the courtroom. Offended by Loesch's show of disrespect, Guenther shouted: "All that Loesch craves is his name in the paper every day. I want to answer his tirade and ——"

"That will be enough," the judge said. "Severance granted."[29]

Delays and Difficulties

On the day of the trial of Boss Morris Eller's henchmen, the benches in the front of the courtroom filled up first with seventeen hard-looking guys. They wore pale green shirts, tan shoes, and sporty ties. When a small, round, gray fellow with a mustache entered the courtroom, several of the defendants got to their feet, others straightened up, and a few walked over to the man. Morris Eller. The boss. Eller sat down on the end of one of the front benches like the end man in an old-fashioned minstrel show. Eller sat with his boys.

The courtroom filled up. The back rows of benches were covered with an unobtrusive file of middle-class men called in for jury service. Most of their faces were vaguely troubled. Their brows were furled. Excuses were being summoned. Big lawyers appeared. Frank J. Loesch appeared small, tanned, with a gray circle of hair. David Stansbury, his chief assistant, stayed close to Loesch. Prosecutor Benedict J. Short thumb-holed his vest, suggesting he was a movie-type lawyer. Thomas D. Nash, one of the attorneys for the defense, had the gray-haired, distinguished appearance of a magazine-ad attorney.

Then Judge O'Connor entered and seated himself squarely, like a teacher on the first day of school facing a new class. His voice was small, clipped, decided. He made a little talk to the veniremen, telling them it was one of their duties as citizens "to serve on a jury once in a while." He knew what was coming next. Presently, he ordered all those who thought they had excuses to come forward. Almost half of the prospective jurors came up to the bench. One was a brother-in-law of an attorney in the case. That let him out. Another said he had fainting spells, and so it went for the next three weeks, the time devoted to examining over 300 veniremen.[30]

Finally, on October 12 the defense and prosecution agreed on the final juror, and the clerk of court said to the entire jury: "Gentlemen, rise and be sworn." As the jurors rose, they began to clap and cheer, glad apparently that the trial proper was due to get under way.[31]

On October 13, Edwin J. Raber, assistant special prosecutor, charged in his opening arguments that Morris Eller offered to furnish his followers with guns with which to terrorize and intimidate voters and poll watchers on April 10, 1928. Raber told the jury that Eller gathered his henchmen at his ward headquarters at 1252 South Halsted Street on the night before the April 10 primary. Raber quoted Eller as follows:

> This election must be won at all costs. If you don't win this election, you're through. If you need guns, you can get them at
> Johnny Armondo's home. (Armondo was one of the henchmen on

trial.) Don't look for trouble. Don't drink any whisky tonight. Do all your drinking after the election. We have got to win. We have the governor and the state's attorney. The police won't interfere.[32]

After this dramatic start, the trial of Eller's henchmen dragged on for two months as the prosecutors called witness after witness. Difficulties, however, stymied the prosecution's forward motion. One of the prosecution's witnesses who saw the Granady murder was slain to prevent him from talking;[33] a second prosecution witness was assaulted; a third witness was nearly the victim of a kidnapping plot;[34] and a fourth witness was offered a bribe of a $175-a-month job if he would recant testimony given to the special grand jury.[35]

To make matters worse, all the money in the privately subscribed fund of $150,000 had been spent, so there was no more money left to pay Loesch and his staff. Irritating Loesch even more was his own personal misfortune. Stepping out of a taxi at the posh Drake Hotel where he lived, Loesch slipped and fractured a bone in his left ankle. The accident confined him to bed for two weeks, but Loesch continued to conduct his campaign on political corruption and gangsters from his hotel suite.[36]

Mixing Politics with Prosecutions

Loesch took a hiatus from his work as special prosecutor on November 3 to advocate the candidacy of John A. Swanson for state's attorney in the general election. One judge on the criminal court took exception to Loesch's mixing of reform politics with criminal prosecutions. Judge John Sullivan complained from the bench that "Loesch has given the investigation of election crimes a political tinge." Sullivan said he would refuse to allow Loesch's investigation as an adjunct to any man's candidacy for state's attorney or for any other political office.[37]

On election eve the injured Loesch addressed Cook County voters over the radio from his hotel suite. "Judge Swanson," Loesch said slowly as he began the broadcast, "has had unusual public experience. He has been a member of the legislature, a Municipal court judge, and now for seven years a judge of the Circuit court. Thus, he has had administrative, legislative, and judicial experience, all of which are aids to a state's attorney."

Loesch told his listeners that the state's attorney was the most powerful officer in Cook County and that an honest state's attorney could do more in cleaning up the corrupt political and criminal conditions in the county than all the other law enforcement agencies put together. "In Swanson," Loesch said, "lies the only hope left of a cleanup of crime in Chicago, which will present to the world in 1933 a different Chicago from what it is today." Loesch said that unless Swanson was elected "all the good work done by the special grand juries will be lost." He warned voters not to lose the benefits of the revolt in the April primary in which Swanson was nominated with a majority of more than 200,000 votes. "Now is the time to follow through by putting him into office."

A newspaper reporter, present in Loesch's suite during this radio talk, noted that Loesch appeared strong as he leaned back into his wheelchair, his hands folded across his tan dressing robe. He wore a linen collar with a blue silk cravat. His chin and jaws were set firmly, and he looked straight in front of him with studious eyes, as if he were seeing Judge Swanson and Judge Lindsay, the two candidates for state's attorney, side by side, against a wall of the room.

"I have no feeling about Judge Lindsay, the Democratic candidate for state's attorney," Loesch told his radio listeners. "But I am satisfied he would not be permitted by people supporting him to carry out the pledges he is making. My conviction is based on the fact that the Crowe-Eller crowd, although in the Republican party, are all supporting Lindsay who is a Democrat. He, therefore, would be under such an obligation to them, and they would have such control over him that he would not be permitted to make any necessary changes in the state's attorney's office." Loesch explained to his audience that he was making political recommendations because voters had deluged him with requests for information as to how they could smash the crime ring and its political allies.

Turning his attention to the office of coroner, Loesch appealed to voters to elect Dr. Herman N. Bundesen. Bundesen was running against Oscar Wolff, the incumbent, whom Loesch had previously described as "that amazingly incompetent man." "Bundesen should be elected coroner," Loesch said. "He is a man of wide reputation, a man of knowledge and integrity. The coroner is an important official in the fight against crime. He should be surrounded by competent officials so that the state's attorney may be apprised of the facts in homicide cases. Oscar Wolff is the most asinine official I have ever come in contact with. He is surrounded by inefficient men."[38]

Loesch saw in this election a chance to complete the job Chicago voters had begun in the April primary and to wipe out almost the last vestiges of the old Thompson machine from power. Only a half dozen of the candidates of the old city hall gang were still facing the voters' pencils; the rest of the gang had dropped into obscurity at the April primary. Standing out from under the shadow of the contest between Al Smith and Herbert Hoover for president was a battle royal between Judge Swanson and Judge Lindsay for state's attorney. Judge Swanson's supporters had rallied around the Republican nominee many organizations of independent voters and numerous church and civic organizations. Yet, Swanson's boosters had been handicapped by the action of State's Attorney Crowe who had urged his Republican followers to knife fellow Republican Swanson and throw every vote to Lindsay, the Democrat.

An Unholy Alliance

Fearing a repeat of the murder, fraud, kidnappings, and sluggings that marred the April primary, Loesch felt compelled to do something drastic to insure a free, honest election. He arranged to secretly meet with Al Capone. For a man of Loesch's stature, this was a galling mission because he was committed to destroy the man whose aid he sought.

When Loesch reached Capone's headquarters at the Lexington Hotel, he found Capone in an officelike room with a half dozen of his non-English-speaking guards standing with their hands on their guns. Over Capone's desk hung oil portraits of George Washington, Abraham Lincoln, and "Big Bill" Thompson. The thought that someone would place two great presidents alongside a buffoon like Thompson flabbergasted Loesch, but he got down to business with Capone immediately. Loesch asked the gangster how long he expected "to beat the law." Capone replied that he would "always beat the law, but die at the business end of a shotgun. But they'll only get me when I'm not looking."

Capone asked Loesch what he wanted. The president of the Crime

Commission told him that he was concerned about the coming election. The arch-criminal then had the effrontery to tell Loesch that he would give Loesch a square deal if Loesch did not ask too much of him.

"Now look here, Capone," said Loesch. "We want an honest election. Will you help by keeping your damned cutthroats and hoodlums from interfering with the voting?"

"Sure," said Scarface Al. "I'll give them the works, because they are all Dagos up there, but what about the Salitis gang of Micks over on the west side? They'll have to be handled different. Do you want me to give them the works, too?"

Impressed with Capone's willingness to help suppress the gangs on the west side, Loesch expressed his gratitude.

"All right," Capone said, "I'll have the cops send over the squad cars the night before the election and jug all the hoodlums and keep in them in the cooler until the polls close."

Loesch extended his hand and the two men shook.[39]

Capone kept his word. On the eve of the election, Chicago police spread a dragnet, rounding up and disarming many known gangsters. It did not come as a surprise to Loesch when, on election eve, he received word that seventy squad cars had gone out and seized roughnecks. Balloting proceeded without disorder. "It turned out to be the squarest and most successful election in forty years," Loesch said later in a lecture at the Southern California Academy of Criminology. "There was not one complaint, not one election fraud and no threat of trouble all day."[40]

Chicago voters did what Loesch had hoped for. They smashed the worn-out old Thompson-Crowe machine to flinders. Not a single one of the six candidates of that machine who had survived the primary of April 10 succeeded in escaping the voters' wrath at the election of November 6. The "last ditchers" among the Thompsonites, Morris Eller, Coroner Wolff, and four others, were beaten badly, unable to ride to victory even in a general Republican triumph.

Eller, the Twentieth Ward boss, who was awaiting trial on criminal charges, suffered perhaps the most startling defeat of any of the Thompson-Crow candidates. Eller had squeaked past the primary with a seriously questioned margin of a few thousand votes and had hoped to be pulled through to a seat for another six years on Chicago's sanitary district by a local victory for Herbert Hoover. Hoover furnished the victory in Cook County, but Eller was scarcely able to garner the vote of one in five persons who cast ballots in the sanitary district election.[41]

Quite as symptomatic of the anti-Thompsonism in this election, former Health Commissioner Bundesen, discarded by Thompson before his third term had gone very far, was elected coroner on the Democratic ticket by the largest plurality polled by anybody. And finally, the voters elected Judge John Swanson, who had defeated Crowe in the Republican primary, state's attorney by a majority of more than 140,000 votes over Judge William J. Lindsay, Democrat.

Loesch, elated at these results, took out the following ad in the *Daily News*:

> The terrific defeat given to the Thompson machine means wonders for Chicago. By the election, Chicago has shown that it means to clean house; that it means to have honest, decent, and peaceful elections. It will present to the world in the next four years a city of which every self-respecting citizen shall be proud. A new day for Chicago has dawned.[42]

Convictions Without Just Punishment

On November 23, 1928, a jury found Boss Ellers's seventeen henchmen guilty of various conspiracies, the principal ones of which were conspiracy to murder, kidnap, assault, and intimidate voters during the orgy of lawlessness in the Twentieth Ward at the April tenth primary. The same jury imposed punishment on the henchmen, meting out fines that ranged from $1,250 down to $400.[43]

Frank Loesch, who had been in charge of the prosecution, regarded the punishment as too lenient. Talking to reporters at his suite in the Drake Hotel, Loesch said, "The offenses committed were so serious that fines are not a just punishment. The verdict and the judgement constitute an apology to these men for having tried them. Eller's henchmen escaped what they deserved—imprisonment."[44]

David D. Stansbury, Loesch's first assistant in the prosecution, saw red. "What's the use of discussing it? I can't say anything about it without using words that would not be printable." After a pause he added, "And they're planning to hold a world's fair here in 1933."[45]

Harry Eugene Kelly, an attorney who had promoted the special grand jury investigation, interpreted the verdict as being the result of a belief on the part of the jury that the men on trial were merely the tools of the Ellers, father and son, and that the Ellers were yet to be tried.[46]

Disappointed, but with no thoughts of quitting, Loesch pledged to drive "Scarface Al" and other gangsters out of Chicago. In a speech given at the Woman's City Club of Chicago on the day after the jury's verdict, Loesch revealed that the special grand jury would make a "whirlwind drive" against the last remaining stronghold of the hoodlums in Chicago—the police department. Referring to the police assigned to patrol the polls on primary day, April 10, 1928, Loesch said, "The police at the polls saw nothing, heard nothing, and knew nothing. The biggest single thing state's attorney-elect Swanson can do is to clean up the police force." Turning to his favorite topic, which was good citizenship, Loesch said: "Ladies, change has come. Do you remember that beautiful statue at Chicago's last world's fair, representing the spirit of Chicago, the spirit that means 'I Will'? That spirit has returned."[47]

New Life for the Inquiry

Tempering Loesch's optimism was the fact that his appointment as assistant attorney general in charge of the election inquiry was about to expire on December 3. State's Attorney Swanson pumped new life into the election inquiry, however, on November 27, 1929. Swanson made Loesch an assistant state's attorney and assigned him the duty of carrying on the drive to rid Chicago of "politico-criminal alliances."

Under the new arrangement, Loesch retained the same post he had held for the past six months, that of special prosecutor of the inquiry into the relationship of certain politicians to the underworld, and he continued to work with the same staff. In discussing the details of the deal with Loesch, Swanson said, "The new setup will mean a financial sacrifice to every man on Loesch's staff, but Loesch has inspired his aids with such confidence and respect as to make them willing to undergo a sacrifice to complete the job of cleaning up Chicago."[48]

Before Loesch could resume work under a new boss, seven members of "Bugs" Moran's gang were gunned down on February 14,

1929. Police Commissioner William Russell proclaimed "a war to the finish" with Capone and promised to make the massacre "the death knell of gangdom." Based on his own bad experiences in dealing with the Chicago police as a special prosecutor, Loesch realized that Russell was making empty promises.

While speaking at a convocation at the University of Chicago one month after the massacre, Loesch put it bluntly: "There can be no great help from the police as long as they are controlled by Mayor Thompson who is allied with Al Capone. When the source is polluted, the stream is tainted all the way." Touching specifically on the massacre, Loesch remarked that it was an amazing feat to slaughter seven men at one time in daylight in a congested portion of the city and escape immediate arrest. According to Loesch, the murderers must have thought that they would be protected. At the end of his speech, Loesch preached citizenship to the graduates. "The law is a living fact, but it is not self-executing," he said. "It needs the human touch to vitalize it. That means you and me as well as law-enforcing officers. Whether or not the law triumphs in Chicago will depend not upon mere good will, but upon actual work which every one of us must do to fight crime."[49]

Enlisting President Hoover in the Crusade

Practicing what he had preached to the University of Chicago graduates, Loesch led a committee of prominent Chicago citizens to Washington, D.C., to urge President Herbert Hoover to step up federal efforts to incapacitate Al Capone. The businessmen met with Hoover in March 1929. They told him that Chicago was in the hands of gangsters, that the police and magistrates were completely under the gangsters' control, that appealing to the governor of Illinois was futile, and that the federal government was the only force by which the city's ability to govern itself could be restored.[50]

Hoover promised Loesch and the other businessmen that he would "get Capone." At once he directed all federal agencies to concentrate upon Capone and his allies. Thereafter, Hoover kept constant pressure on Andrew Mellon, secretary of the Treasury, to go after Capone. Mellon described morning sessions at the White House during which President Hoover and cabinet members limbered up by tossing a medicine ball around. Mellon said, "When the exercising starts, Mr. Hoover says, 'Have you got that fellow Capone yet?' And when exercising is done and everybody is leaving, the last thing Mr. Hoover always says is: 'Remember, now; I want that man Capone in jail.' "[51]

The Magic Barrel Case

Back in Chicago, a Loesch-led grand jury indicted thirteen of the original defendants for kidnapping and assault to kill Russell B. Sampson, a Chicago Bar Association poll watcher. Under this indictment, a jury, upon rendering a trial guilty verdict, would be required to inflict prison sentences. The second trial was a stormy one in which both prosecution and defense witnesses were charged with perjury; some of them were jailed. On April 20, 1929, the jury returned a verdict acquitting all thirteen defendants.[52]

Loesch rushed more indictments through the grand jury, thus commencing another trial. The third trial established the crude, audacious methods used to commit election frauds in the Twenty-seventh Ward during the 1928 primary. This was the "magic barrel case" that got its name from a pickle barrel, used to hold votes, which sprouted 400 additional ballots after the polls had closed on April 10, 1928.

August Scholz, one of the participants in a plot to give 400 extra ballots to candidates on the Thompson ticket, took the stand as a witness for the state and made a clean breast of how vote fraud was carried out. Scholz explained that he and several of the other defendants, while well fortified with moonshine, spent primary eve marking Republican ballots for the Thompson ticket and Democratic ballots for a fellow named Auth, who was running for state representative. The next day they put the fraudulent ballots into a pickle barrel that sat in a corner of the polling place at 672 West Monroe Street.

Just before the polls closed, one of the defendants stole the poll book so there would be no official record of how many votes had been cast at that polling spot. After the polls closed, another one of the defendants emptied the ballot box into the pickle barrel. But a poll watcher, who had jotted down the names of every person who had voted in a book, foiled the plot. By the poll watcher's count, 315 persons had voted. When this poll watcher emptied the magic barrel, he discovered 715 ballots.

All ten defendants tried for ballot frauds in the Eleventh Precinct of the Twenty-seventh Ward at the 1928 primary were found guilty by a jury. Five of the magic barrel defendants drew prison sentences from six months to a year in addition to fines. Most of the men found guilty were supporters of Homer K. Galpin, who, as chairman of the Central Committee of the Cook County Republican Party, campaigned to elect Thompsonites. One of the defendants was State Senator James B. Leonardo, who had already been found guilty and fined $750 at the first trial on a conspiracy charge.[53]

Loesch charged forward with a fourth trial. This one opened with Loesch accusing thirteen Eller henchmen with kidnapping and assault. Specifically, they were charged with kidnapping two poll watchers from the voting place in the First Precinct, carrying them to 1352 South Peoria Street, holding them captive there until 10 P.M., and beating them. Kidnapping and assault charges against nine of the Eller henchmen were dropped on April 24. For the four who remained, it was the their third trial. They had been convicted by a jury at the first trial in the fall but drew only fines.

After less than three hours of deliberation on May 22, in which seven ballots were taken, the jury acquitted Senator Leonardo, Sam Kaplan, John Armondo, and Rocco Fanelli. This was the second time within a month that the same four men had been acquitted of crimes committed during the primary election of April 10, 1928. This verdict presaged the end of the prosecution of the so-called Eller henchmen for crimes charged against them in the Twentieth and Twenty-seventh wards, the former under control of the elder Eller and the latter the bailiwick of Homer Galpin, chairman of the Central Committee of the Cook County Republican Party, who dodged Loesch and all seven of the special grand juries for more than one year.

As for City Collector Morris Eller and his son Judge Emanuel Eller of the criminal court, the special prosecutor's cases against them never reached the trial stage. The Ellers faced conspiracy charges in connection with wholesale vote frauds, kidnappings, and one murder in the "bloody" Twentieth Ward during the April 1928 primary, but when Loesch announced he was not prepared to go to trial, those charges were dismissed in court on May 21 and May 22. Loesch asked for a sixty-day continuance on the grounds that two important witnesses had disappeared. Thomas D. Nash, the Ellers's counsel, argued that, under "the four term rule," the cases must proceed at once, as the state already had four continuances. The judge agreed with Nash and, upon hearing Loesch admit he was unprepared to proceed with the trial of the two Ellers, dismissed charges against both.

As soon as Morris Eller reached the outer corridor of the courtroom, he exploded with wrath over the insistence of the state in bringing charges against his son and him. "Just playing politics—that's all it is," he declared.[54]

A Split over Tactics

Bitter disagreement developed between Loesch and State's Attorney Swanson over prosecution tactics for fighting crime. Loesch favored continuing to prosecute politicians and their henchmen who conspired to thwart free elections in Chicago. State's Attorney Swanson, however, became preoccupied with the peccadillos, habits, and misdemeanors of parts of the population victimized by organized crime. Swanson's obsession was with dog races and betting on them, with slot machines, bunko parlors, poolrooms, beer flats, card games—irregularities and vices in the sight of the law—but not murder, robbery, or election frauds. From Loesch's point of view, justice seemed hopeless of success while this flailing of petty vice occupied the attention and consumed the activity of the state's attorney and the police.[55]

Two examples, both of which happened on the night of June 11, illustrate that point. In the first example, thirty squads of detectives raided three dog tracks on the outskirts of Chicago, closing the tracks, arresting more than 100 employees, and sending home customers. The raids were under the supervision of Patrick Roche, chief investigator for State's Attorney Swanson, who termed them "a smashing blow at the murdering gangsters of Chicago and Cook County." The tracks closed in this raid were the Laramie Kennel Club, 35th Street and 52nd Avenue, Cicero, owned by the Capone syndicate, with Edward J. O'Hare as president; the Illinois Kennel Club, 175th and Halsted streets, owned by the Chicago Heights ring with Homer Ellis as president; and the Fairview Kennel Club, Lawrence Avenue and Mannheim Road, opened by the "Bugs" Moran gang, with William J. O'Brien as figurehead.[56]

That same night the love of Frankie and Johnnie proved to be too hot for State's Attorney Swanson and the police. Emissaries of State's Attorney Swanson and Police Commissioner William Russell looked with disapproving eyes upon the stage version of the maudlin old ballad, which a press agent had called "as snappy as a new garter; as natural as a seven eleven." Prosecutors and police officers, who viewed the production at the Adelphi Theater, took the position that Chicago's morals would benefit by banning this show from the city. Police warned the manager of the show that a police detail would be present at the theater the next night to prevent the curtain from going up. Police Commissioner Russell reported that the police had received numerous complaints about the show. Many people in Chicago, according to Russell, objected to the torrid stage romance of Johnnie, the country boy, out for a hot time in the big city, and the painted ladies on the St. Louis levee in the days of 1849.[57]

The futility of the authorities' efforts to regulate people's morals became apparent the next day. At the three dog tracks in Cook County, dogs were chasing electric rabbits again thanks to a temporary injunction issued by Judge Harry M. Fisher in circuit court. This injunction restrained the state's attorney's office, the police department, and the sheriff from making "unlawful arrests" or unlawfully interfering with the operations of the tracks.[58]

As for Frankie and Johnnie, the ending wasn't so sweet—at least from the point of view of the actors who found themselves unromantically out of jobs. Interviewed in her dressing room, Georgie Kern, who had the part of the hard-talking, straight-shooting Frankie, looked pained when told that the state's attorney was closing her show because she was corrupting the morals of the citizens of Chicago. "There's nothing wrong with the play—except that these characters were girls of the levee, and they dance with men, and drink with them. What's wrong with a story about a girl, who falls in love with a man named Johnnie, and finally shoots him?"[59]

Loesch's Last Trial

State's Attorney Swanson pulled out of Loesch's election inquiry and stripped Loesch of his staff and resources. Nevertheless, Loesch made a last stand. He persuaded a special grand jury on October 11 to indict police Lieutenant Philip Carroll, four other detectives, and three of Eller's henchmen for the murder of Octavius Granady.

Before that trial, authorities stood divided concerning the guilt of Lieutenant Carroll and three members of his squad. Loesch swore he had fourteen witnesses who would testify that Carroll and his men were involved in a wild chase through the streets that ended when Granady fled from his automobile and was shot down. Deputy Commissioner John Stege, who, after being reinstated on the police force, had left Loesch's team of investigators, disagreed. He said a "terrible mistake" was being made in the case of Carroll and that Carroll could not possibly have had any connection with the killing. Sheridan Brusseaux, a well-known black private detective who had assisted in Loesch's investigation of Granady's murder, said he had never found any facts to indicate Carroll had any hand in the shooting.[60]

On October 19, one of the chief witnesses against Carroll was shot to death in a lover's quarrel that was apparently unrelated to the case.[61] A bad omen came on October 25 when the stock market crashed, creating a climate of bewilderment and uncertainty in Chicago and across the nation. The trial, which started on November 18, turned out to be a farce.

On the second day of the trial, a prosecution witness who had assured Loesch before the trial that he had seen John Armondo, one of the defendants, shooting at Granady's car, changed his story. On direct examination from Loesch, this witness refused to identify John Armondo as one of the men who had fired bullets at Granady. On cross-examination he even said Armondo was not the man who was shooting.

Another state's witness told an entirely new version of the Octavius Granady murder in court on November 20. Giving an eyewitness account of the murder, Bryant McDonald said he was standing in front of the polls at 1222 Blue Island Avenue around five o'clock in the evening when he saw a little man walk out into the street, pull a gun out of his pocket, and shoot at Granady's car as it passed by. McDonald also said he saw a uniformed policeman run out, grab the man with the gun, and surrender him to three men in plain clothes who came up and flashed stars. When the judge asked McDonald if either the man with the gun or the police officers he saw were present in the courtroom, McDonald shook his head and said they were not.[62]

The Granady murder trial reached uproarious heights the following day when Julius Mayo, a state's witness, identified a defense attorney as one of the gunmen who had fired shots at Granady. This misidentification sparked a roar of laughter from the spectators. Carroll and eight other defendants, four of whom were policemen, smiled broadly. Loesch protested to the judge, the jury looked confused, and the judge cried to the grinning defense attorney, "They've got you at last, Milton."[63] Mayo was followed on the witness stand by another state's witness, Roosevelt Mazck, who was positive in his identification of Carroll as an occupant of the squad car that pursued the Granady car. Cross-examination brought out, however, that an employee of the state's attorney's office had procured a job in the washroom of the Union League club for Mazck in exchange for his promise to testify in the trial.

Margaret Welch, yet another witness for the prosecution, caused the biggest outburst of the trial. Heralded as a star witness for the state, she fell on her knees before the judge, raised her hands to heaven, and shrieked that she could not testify. She had been about to commit perjury, she confessed. Defense attorneys rushed forward with cries that the witness had been bribed to commit perjury for the state. They exclaimed that they had proof that she was to receive $1,500 for her testimony. Prosecutor Loesch made an indignant denial, but so much damage had been done to the prosecution's case that Loesch nol-prossed the murder charges against two of the eight defendants against whom Welch was to have testified, James Belcastro and John Armondo.[64]

On November 26 the circus-like trial continued with Loesch tilting with Judge Joseph B. David. When the seventy-seven-year-old special prosecutor defied Judge David's recommendation that murder charges against Lieutenant Carroll and five other defendants be dismissed, the judge declared that Loesch had been the dupe of crooked investigators and perjured witnesses. Loesch retorted that the court had shown "a partial and meddlesome attitude" since the beginning of the trial.

"I'll let you go ahead, then," yelled Judge David. "But if there is a verdict of guilty, I'll set it aside."

"Your attitude in this case is unprecedented in the annals of judicial history of Cook County!" shouted Loesch.

Later in the day the judge and the special prosecutor confronted one another again. The testimony of Helen Madigan, a state witness who became confused and contradicted herself at various times, caused a wrangle.

After sending the jury out, Judge David said to Loesch: "Is there anybody on earth gullible enough to believe that woman's story?"

"I do," returned Loesch tartly.

"Then try to make the jury believe it," advised the judge.

"I will," said Loesch.

"I think that woman is the most unmitigated liar that ever was on a witness stand," declared Judge David.

"Everybody is a liar that identifies Carroll under your interpretation," retorted the special prosecutor.

"Most of them are," shouted the judge.

"Most of them are not," returned Loesch in just as loud a voice. "You are condemned as a partial judge." "The trouble with you, Mr. Loesch," replied the judge, "is that you have deliberately manufactured a case against these police officers."

Another squabble broke out during the afternoon session that turned the air blue and made the first tilt appear mild. Judge David advised the defense lawyers not to present any evidence, but they insisted on putting in their side of the case. Defense attorneys W. W. Smith and Milton Smith set off fireworks by calling two witnesses who had been subpoenaed by the state but who had not been used. These witnesses told a story exonerating Lieutenant Carroll. Jack Feller, a timid little man, by occupation a butcher, was the center of the afternoon explosion. He was an eyewitness of the murder that occurred at 13th Street and Hoyne Avenue. He testified that Lieutenant Carroll and his squad did not arrive on the scene until ten minutes after the killing. Examination brought out that the state knew Feller's story but chose not to call him to the witness stand. Judge David, who had been fuming since the morning outburst, questioned Feller. His queries brought out that Feller knew none of the principals in the case and was a disinterested witness.

"Why didn't you call him to the stand?" the judge demanded of the special prosecutor. "In his testimony he overshadows ninety percent of the state's witnesses. It's your duty to call all witnesses, no matter if the evidence is adverse to the state's case."

Prosecutor Loesch started to speak, but the judge ordered: "Take out the jury."

When the jurors had retired, Judge David began to speak softly at first, then increasingly louder until his voice was booming. "Gentlemen of the state's attorney's office," he said, "the court recommends that you enter a nolle prosse in this case against all the defendants. The more I see of this case, the more the attitude of the state displeases me."

Trembling with anger, Loesch rose from his seat and pointed a finger at the judge. "I shall speak for the state," he said loudly. "We shall do nothing of the kind."

The following colloquy ensued:

Defense Attorney Milton Smith: We don't want to nolle prosse the case.

Judge David: I don't care what you want. I am tired of wasting time in this case.

Loesch: If your honor would do less talking, we wouldn't waste so much time.

Judge David: You don't talk to me that way. You are an old man and respect is due you, but ——.

Loesch: All right, all right.

Judge David: I have been patient with you.

Loesch: And I've been patient with you, too.

Judge David: . . . and listened to your abuse. I respect your age and standing at the bar, but in this case, sir, you are all wrong. You have not taken the position of an impartial prosecutor, and your attitude is not one of desiring to see justice done. You have put witnesses on the stand who are so guilty of perjury that it smells to heaven. Your case is so weak there is no excuse in going on.[65]

"Fighting a Dragon"

Following eight days of the trial, with at least one sensational scene featured each day in court, the ending was anticlimactic. On November 27, Judge David, acting on a motion by Loesch, dismissed the case against Lieutenant Carroll and six others charged with the murder of Octavius Granady. In demanding that the trial be terminated, Loesch asserted that Judge David had "heaped abuse on witnesses and counsel for the state" and had made it "intolerable" to go on. Judge David declined to answer Loesch's accusations but admitted he might have been hasty in making some judgments. Dismissal of the case meant that Loesch had twice failed to convict anyone of the Granady murder.

At the conclusion of the trial, the white-haired veteran of the bar talked with newspaper reporters about his stint as special prosecutor. He admitted he had been only "slightly successful" and proceeded to list these accomplishments: (1) achieving the first honest elections in Chicago history; (2) convicting seventeen Eller henchmen in one case and ten more for stuffing ballot boxes in the magic barrel case; and (3) bringing about the election of an honest state's attorney.

The overall impact of Loesch's work, however, was much larger, for something had happened as a result of Loesch's driving investigation. Knowledge spread that it was dangerous for politicians even to seem to be consorting with crooks; that it was perilous to kill political aspirants; and that it was hazardous to stuff ballot boxes. Gangsters learned that money couldn't buy everything. Loesch disseminated this knowledge through special grand juries, indictments, and prosecutions. He told it directly to politicians. He told it when face to face with Al Capone.[66]

Loesch resigned as special prosecutor on December 1, after more than a year of battling the alliance between crime and politics. Before stepping down, Loesch said: "I knew when I was going after the brotherhood of crime and politics that I was fighting a great dragon. If I haven't beaten him, I tried hard. It's time now for a younger man and new leaders to take up the burden."[67] With respect to Al Capone, Loesch predicted: "If Al Capone is not murdered, the law will get him, or he will die in poverty. He is just as certain to go down as God lives. Don't worry, God's justice will reach every one of the evil gangsters and crooked politicians in our city."[68]

Charles G. Dawes's lobbying of President Coolidge proved to be the real reason that the federal government intervened in the organized crime situation in Chicago. While serving as vice president of the United States from 1925 to 1929, Dawes also pulled strings in Washington, D.C., so honest, aggressive federal prosecutors would be assigned to the Northern District of Illinois to pursue Al Capone.

Frank J. Loesch is seen here in his office at 300 N. Adams, the headquarters of the Chicago Crime Commission. Loesch was often called the "Spirit of '76" because at the age of seventy-six he stepped into the private war against Capone. He battled the Capone gang as a special prosecutor of crimes committed during the Pineapple Primary and as the president of the Chicago Crime Commission.

Burt A. Massee, the foreman of the coroner's jury that investigated the St. Valentine's Day Massacre, is the sixth person from the right in this photograph of the reenactment of the massacre. Massee is the dapper-looking man standing next to the man with the bow tie and horn-rimmed glasses. In response to the mass slaying of seven men on February 14, 1929, he founded the Scientific Crime Detection Laboratory at Northwestern University and enlisted Calvin H. Goddard in the crusade against Al Capone.

Calvin H. Goddard was a premier ballistics expert who came to Chicago from New York to solve the St. Valentine's Day Massacre. Even though Goddard produced scientific evidence linking Fred ("Killer") Burke to the massacre, no one was ever prosecuted for the killing of "Bugs" Moran's men on Valentine's Day. Goddard went on to become the first director of the Scientific Crime Detection Laboratory, a privately funded lab that the city of Chicago purchased in 1938.

Henry Barrett Chamberlin, the operating director of the Chicago Crime Commission from 1919 to 1942, labeled Al Capone "Public Enemy Number One." Chamberlin's public enemies drive stigmatized gangsters and energized some law enforcement authorities to go after Capone and his henchmen.

Colonel Robert R. McCormick, the owner of the *Chicago Tribune*, is shown here on the day he testified before the grand jury investigating the Jake Lingle murder in 1930. The gangland killing of Lingle, a *Tribune* reporter, propelled McCormick into the battle against Chicago's gangsters. By underwriting the costs of the investigation into the Lingle case, McCormick avenged the murder of his reporter.

Robert Isham Randolph, an engineer and the president of the Association of Commerce, led one of the strangest gangbusting outfits of all time into combat against Al Capone in 1930. He was the only self-acknowledged member of a group of top-drawer Chicago businessmen that became known as "the Secret Six."

Samuel Insull, a public utilities magnate, bankrolled the Secret Six.
Following Capone's conviction, Insull himself was tried for mail fraud,
embezzlement, and violation of the federal bankruptcy acts. A jury
acquitted him of all charges.

Julius Rosenwald, a great philanthropist and merchant, belonged to the Secret Six.

Edward E. Gore, a public accountant, held joint memberships in the Secret Six and the Chicago Crime Commission.

George A. Paddock, a stockbroker, held joint memberships in the Secret Six and the Chicago Crime Commission. Although Paddock never admitted belonging to the Secret Six, Judge John H. Lyle identified him as a member.

"Scarface Al" Capone *(left)*, the most famous gangster in American history, strikes a classic pose. Here, as was his custom, he allowed a photographer to take a picture of his "good" side. From the perspective of Chicago's business elite, Capone was a supervillain who had to be eliminated if Chicago was to advance toward the goal of becoming the center of culture and civilization.

5

Chicago's Answer to the St. Valentine's Day Massacre

The forces that in the spring primary of 1928 had risen to slay Octavius Granady, to dragoon citizens at the polls, to bomb John Swanson into the state's attorney's office, and to press Frank J. Loesch into service as a special prosecutor rose to smite again. This time they struck with a savagery that Chicago had never seen before.

As a light snow fell on the morning of St. Valentine's Day in 1929, the thermometer registered eighteen above zero in Chicago and there was a westerly wind. At 10:30 in the morning seven men gathered in the garage of the S. M. C. Cartage Company at 2122 North Clark Street in Chicago. Five were members of George ("Bugs") Moran's gang; one was an auto mechanic who worked on the gang's vehicles; and the other was an optometrist who found excitement in hanging around gangsters. The men were waiting for "Bugs" Moran, Willie Marks, and Ted Newberry, who were late.

The night before, Moran had received a telephone call informing him that a truckload of Al Capone's liquor en route from Detroit to Chicago had been hijacked and would be delivered the next day to Moran's beer depot at 2122 North Clark Street. Moran, Marks, and Newberry never reached the garage on the fourteenth because as they approached it they spotted a Cadillac touring car, with curtains drawn, the kind used by police squads in Chicago in the twenties, stop at the curb, two doors north of the garage. They observed five men get out of the automobile—two in police uniforms and three in civilian clothes—and walk to the door and enter. "Coppers," Moran figured, so Moran, Marks, and Newberry decided not to enter the garage until the "heat" was off.

A few minutes later a steady metallic rat-a-tat-tat rang out, then two heavy blasts. The "squad" members emerged from the garage, got into their car, and drove off.[1] Witnesses entering the garage saw a gruesome sight. Six bodies—all riddled with bullets—lay upon the floor by the wall. A single survivor, with a dozen wounds, was dragging himself toward the door. The brick wall where the bodies lay was pocked with bullet marks. Gang member Frank Gusenburg, the lone survivor, lived for three hours and identified his assailants as "cops." When "Bugs" Moran learned of the massacre, he said: "Only Capone kills like that."

This incident was accomplished in eight minutes and was one of the most efficiently planned operations of its kind; it marked a high point in Capone's career, a blow that annihilated the last serious gang opposing his authority.[2] The *Chicago Tribune* showed an insider's perception of the never-to-be-forgotten massacre:

> The gangsters who were killed belonged to the gang of George Moran (whose antagonist) . . . is Al Capone. . . . A more immediate reason lies in a campaign of Moran's alcohol sellers to take liquor from Detroit sources and with it penetrate the Bloody Twentieth Ward, the booze territory of the Capone gang.[3]

Inside the *Tribune*, a photo cutaway depicted the massacre technique, victims lined facing the wall, hands over their heads, killers in cops' uniforms moving by a dotted line from a Cadillac touring car at the curb to a position inside the garage. As reported in the crime story in the *Tribune*, six of the seven were dead when the police arrived; the seventh, Frank Gusenberg, survived briefly to deliver his famous last words. In response to a detective's query, "Who shot you, Frank?" he replied, "Nobody shot me."[4]

The Inquest

Because of the implications of police involvement in the massacre and the spectacular nature of the crime, the Cook County coroner, Dr. Herman N. Bundesen, convened a blue-ribbon coroner's jury. Bundesen wanted the men who conducted the inquest to be capable of appreciating the seriousness of the crime—men whose civic patriotism would prompt them to assist in the apprehension and conviction of the guilty persons.[5] Bundesen selected the following men: Burt A.

Massee, vice president of the Colgate-Palmolive-Peet Company; Walter E. Olson, president of the Olson Rug Company; Major F. J. Streychmans, attorney for the Belgian Consul; Fred Berstein, superior court master in chancery; W. L. Meyer, master in chancery; and Dr. J. V. McCormick, dean of Loyola University's Law School.

The inquest got under way in a dingy patrol room of the Hudson Avenue police station on February 15.[6] Bundesen conducted it with all the formality of a court hearing. Police Commissioner William F. Russell, Detective Chief John Egan, Deputy Commissioner Thomas Wolfe, Captain Thomas Condon of the Hudson Avenue District, and Captain William H. Schoemaker were present for the city. Assistant State's Attorneys Walker Butler and Harry S. Ditchburne were present for the county. Scattered among the spectators were a number of Prohibition agents and other federal officers.

For a reenactment of the massacre, the inquest moved to the garage on North Clark Street where death had been meted out. Sergeant Thomas Burke and a police squad took the roles of the slain members of the Moran gang. They faced the wall, their hands in the air. Coroner Bundesen stood to one side, and the coroner's physician, E. L. Benjamin, stood at the other. Nearly 200 bullets were fired, the physician indicated, and more than 100 of them found their marks. Some of the victims had as many as 20 bullets and slugs in their bodies. As Dr. Benjamin talked, the jurors gazed about at the blood-stained floor, interrupting periodically to ask questions.

This scene in the garage that served as a beer depot for the Moran gang was almost as incredible as the gang massacre the day before. The coroner's jury of business and professional men tramped with their well-polished boots on the spots where dead gangsters had lain, and solemnly watched the reenactment. Staring the jurymen in their faces was a gray brick wall, as forbidding as any against which condemned men have ever been stoned, chipped where the rain of bullets struck it—the chipped places smeared. They couldn't help but notice a chair—one of the rungs broken by bullet-fire—across which Frank Gusenberg's body had lain as the blood poured from his wounds. More dark stains in the stone floor were partly hidden by the feet of police officers and reporters as they crowded in the narrow spaces between the huge beer trucks at the east end of the garage. A beer flat, ready to be put up, with the iron bands piled beside it, was lying on one of the trucks. A huge brown and gray police dog, tethered in the dim west end of the garage, howled eerily above the voice of the coroner's physician while he was outlining the manner in which each of the seven met his death.

"And here," droned the coroner's physician, indicating with his thumb a point on the torso of the lay figure for a dead gangster, "is the flattened jacket of a steel-jacketed bullet, imbedded three and one-half-inches." He described the manner in which the bullets had entered the bodies of the dead men.

The coroner's jury stood about solemnly, listening. Newspaper photographers and reporters were perched atop a beer truck to get a better view of the action. Commissioner Russell, in a dark overcoat and white muffler, passed in and out of the garage, while Captain William Schoemaker chewed on the stub of a cigar. Burt Massee, president of the Palmolive company and jury foreman, attired in a gray suit and a derby hat, listened intently; Felix J. Streychmans, a member of the jury, sat on a pile of lumber against the wall. Captain Condon of the Hudson Avenue station and a dozen other police officers guarded the door against the curious crowd that had gathered outside. Such a scene reproduced on a stage in a drama would have been labeled unreal or overdone. Too much blood and too many bullets. Too great a contrast between the well-tailored coroner's jury and the hoodlums whose murders they were investigating.[7]

Blaming the Police

In a gesture of support for Bundesen's jury, the Chicago Association of Commerce (CAC) posted a $50,000 reward for information leading to the arrest and conviction of the killers. An aroused public added $10,000 more. The city council and the state's attorney's office added $20,000 each, bringing the total to $100,000.

Commenting on the impact of the massacre on business, a spokesman for the CAC said: "Naturally, the Association of Commerce is vitally concerned with the damage an event like this will have on the reputation and business connections of our city."[8] The same spokesman called for:

1. An immediate grand jury investigation of the crime and any possible police department connection to it

2. The prompt implementation of the recommendations for reorganization of the police department with particular emphasis on such provisions as would prevent the selection of new policemen on any basis other than merit

3. The establishment of cooperation between all law enforcing agencies of the state, the county, and the city to discover and punish those guilty of committing the massacre

4. Cooperation with federal law enforcement agencies[9]

State's Attorney Swanson blamed the Chicago police. Swanson scored the police for failing to destroy the gangsters' rich sources of revenue—booze-selling, gambling, racketeering, and prostitution—which engendered deadly feuds, organized banditry, and systematic corruption.

Walter Strong, the editor and publisher of the *Chicago Daily News*, sided with the business leaders and Swanson.

It is idle for the police to plead helplessness. For the shameful truth is known—not a few so-called guardians of law and order are in the pay of the professional criminals who are shielded and protected also by politicians of certain types in and out of public office. Crime and lawlessness long have flourished in Chicago and the chief cause of the discreditable situation is to be found in the city hall and its affiliated agencies of unscrupulous spoilsmanship."[10]

So much pressure was brought to bear on the police department that Chicago, for a while, became a closed and dry town as the city's fifty-five hundred policemen scurried about the city, bearing orders from their deputy commissioners and captains, that all speakeasies, stills, and breweries must cease operations. Police Commissioner William F. Russell acted under instructions from Mayor Thompson, who was reportedly "horrified" by the gang massacre. Thompson's order to Russell to crack down resulted from a meeting held on February 15 at which State's Attorney Swanson demanded that the police and the Cook County sheriff clean up booze dives and vice dens.[11]

Owners and patrons of drinking establishments agreed that the killings had sounded the death knell of lax Prohibition enforcement in Chicago. To add to the woes of bootleggers, drinkers, and others involved in the illicit marketplace set up by Prohibition, special agents of the Prohibition department seized a truckload of Canadian whiskey in front of 227 West Chicago Avenue, just a block from the Chicago Avenue police station. The whiskey had just been driven into Chicago from Detroit.

Police Commissioner Russell tried to put to rest the insinuations that corruption in the police department—collusion between officers and politicians and speakeasy owners—was responsible for the conditions that led up to the gang butchery. Addressing newsmen, Russell said: "If any of you have any evidence against any policeman in connection with these murders, give that evidence to me. If you can bring such evidence, the proper action will be taken. It won't make any difference whether the man is even a captain or a deputy commissioner—he will be prosecuted."[12]

A Chain of Evidence

On February 22, a fire broke out in the garage behind a house at 1723 North Wood Street, about three miles west of the garage where the massacre took place. Police found a black Cadillac touring car and traced it to a Michigan Avenue car dealer, who said he had sold it to "James Foster." From the owner of the Wood Street property, police discovered that a "Frank Rogers" rented the garage on February 7. He gave 1859 West North Avenue as his address. When the police checked the house at that address, they found it deserted and learned that it adjoined the Circus Cafe, headquarters of Claude Maddox, whose ties to Al Capone were well known.[13]

At the same time, the Chicago police and federal authorities subpoenaed telephone records from the Congress Hotel. Jake Guzik, Capone's financial adviser who occupied a room at the Congress, had been holding daily long-distance conversations with Capone at his Florida villa to within three days of the massacre. Then the calls had ceased, to be resumed again February 18.[14]

On the same day as police found the getaway car, Bundesen used bullet holes to tell the story of the massacre from a coroner's perspective. Using blueprints and charts furnished to him by the two doctors who performed autopsies on the seven dead men, Bundesen said that two machine gunners were stationed on the flanks of the line of men facing the wall. When the machine guns began to crack, the man on the left, according to the doctors' findings, swept across the top of the row of heads. Then the "Tommy man"—Thompson machine gunner—on the right fired a little lower, clipping the necks of the Moranites. Back again each of them came, this time across two lines below both of the previous levels. And then a third time across the knee joints and at the feet, just to speed the helpless victims in falling to the floor. From twenty to fifty bullets were removed from the bodies of each of the seven men, Bundesen stated.

The lineup of the men facing the wall as they "grabbed for the sky" was reconstructed from left to right as follows: Frank Gusenberg, Peter Gusenberg, Al Weinshank, Adam Heyer, James Clark, John May, and Dr. Reinhardt Schwimmer. According to Bundesen, two men armed with shotguns stood between the pair of machine gunners. But only one of them fired. That discharge went to the center of the group, puncturing Heyer's back. May, apparently the most frightened of the group, started to turn his head about to plead for mercy, when a hail of bullets answered his gesture.[15]

One of the machine gunners might have been Capone's favorite triggerman, Jack McGurn. Police arrested McGurn on February 27.[16] The arresting officer seized McGurn at the Hotel Stevens with a pretty blonde named Louise Rolfe. As prosecutors were preparing to place seven charges of murder against McGurn, Al Capone defied a federal grand jury summons ordering him to appear in Chicago on March 12.[17] Authorities indicted McGurn on seven charges of first-degree murder and released him on bail. McGurn's attorneys made four demands for trial, the state asked for four continuances, and finally the state dropped all charges against McGurn.[18]

Capone Dodges the Authorities and Moran

Gangland justice worked faster than criminal justice in the massacre case. "Bugs" Moran vowed revenge, and in a brief time three members of the Capone gang were murdered. They were important killings, for two of the victims were Capone's "choppers," John Scalise and Albert Anselmi. The other was Tony Guinta, a rising young killer. The underworld, however, did not credit Moran, but charged the triple murder to Capone. One account was that Scalise and Anselmi had a plan to double-cross Capone and that Capone, upon discovering their plan, held a dinner party for them during which he smashed in their heads with a baseball bat.

Capone found refuge from both the police and surviving members of the Moran gang at his estate on Palm Island. There he stayed in a comfortable house, which sheltered Capone and his wife and son, his brother Ralph ("Bottles") Capone, and his bodyguards. After the Moran gang massacre, Capone reinforced his garrison, and instead of a dozen guards, Capone and his family were protected by twenty. Eight-foot walls surrounded the estate, and a twenty-four-hour guard watched the front and rear gates.

When a federal grand jury summoned Capone to leave Florida and come back to Chicago on March 12 to answer questions about his Cicero bootlegging business, he feigned illness. "I'm a sick man," Capone told federal authorities on March 4. "Dr. Philips, my physician, is ready to go into federal court in Chicago and tell the judge or the district attorney that I'm too sick to appear. I didn't have anything to do with that shooting up in North Clark Street and there isn't a thing I can tell the police about."[19]

As a "pneumonia convalescent," Capone, according to newspaper reports, had been following the routine of a heavyweight prize-fighter. His program included daily golf, horse racing, and vigorous nightly social activities. In addition, he took boat trips to Nassau and air jaunts to Bimini.[20]

To return to Chicago to answer the grand jury summons, Capone took a circuitous route to evade Moran's hitmen. Leaving his Palm Island estate, Capone motored to New Orleans and took a northbound train to Chicago. With him went Frankie Rio, "Mops" Volpe, and others of his entourage. Upon Capone's arrival at the federal building on March 20, an assistant U.S. district attorney questioned him. Then Capone, accompanied by his attorneys, left the federal building.

"There he is, that's Capone," someone shouted. When a crowd of 500 persons gathered about him and spilled out into the street, Capone's head shrunk into his collar and he started out at a brisk pace. Before he could make his getaway, the crowd gathered around him, jostling him and his attorneys. Capone took off at a lope down the street, dashed into an office building, and disappeared into his attorney's office.

Later that day Capone returned. U.S. Attorney George E. Q. Johnson was sitting in his office in the federal building with a visitor when from the room where Capone was sitting came four explosions. Johnson leaped to his feet. "What is that?" he shouted and rushed into the room. The room was filled with smoke and for a moment the district attorney appeared to believe that there had been a shooting, but then he spied a dozen cameramen taking pictures of Capone.

Johnson observed "Scarface Al," wearing a dark suit, pearl gray spats, and black oxfords. He watched with amazement as numerous persons subjected themselves to being frisked for weapons by U.S. marshals in order to enter the federal building, shake Capone's hand, and inquire about the gangster's health.

Eventually, U.S. marshals took Capone before the grand jury where his attorneys haggled with U.S. district attorneys about what type of immunity might be extended to Capone.[21] Federal authorities continued their pursuit of Capone, and on March 27, a federal court cited Capone for contempt of court for refusing to appear in Chicago on March 12. Capone surrendered after a warrant was issued for his arrest. After furnishing $5,000 bond, he was released only to defy the grand jury again by fleeing to Florida.

Capone ventured away from Florida in May to attend an important conference held at the President Hotel in Atlantic City. From Chicago came Frank Nitti and Frank Rio; from Philadelphia, Max ("Boo Boo") Hoff, Sam Lazar, and Charles Schwartz; from New York, Frank Costello, Lucky Luciano, and Arthur Flegenheimer, alias Dutch Schultz; from Atlantic City, the political boss and racketeer, Enoch J. ("Nucky") Johnson. These gangsters divided the country into spheres of influence. Chicago's north and south side gangs merged under Capone's leadership; the Unione Siciliana reorganized from top to bottom with a new national president. An executive committee, chaired by Torrio, arbitrated all disputes and determined punishment for violations of the agreement.

"Bugs" Moran did not attend the conference. With the remaining members of his gang, he was looking for an opportunity to kill Capone. "Scarface Al" sought refuge in prison.[22]

As soon as the conference ended on May 16, Capone and his bodyguard Frank Rio drove from Atlantic City to Philadelphia where they went to a movie on Market Street. When they came out, two detectives arrested them for carrying concealed weapons. At 11:30

A.M. the following day Capone and Rio entered guilty pleas. A judge imposed the maximum sentence of one year, and Capone was led off with Rio to Philadelphia's Meyamensing prison.[23]

Enter Calvin Goddard

With Capone sealed in prison gloom, Coroner Bundesen continued the inquest into the St. Valentine Day's Massacre. A detective giving testimony to the coroner's jury referred to the cartridges and shells collected from the murder scene. Asked by Burt Massee, the foreman of the jury, what purpose was served by preserving them, the detective explained that with a microscope and various measuring instruments, a ballistics expert could match a bullet with the weapon that fired it. "Unfortunately," the detective added, "the Chicago Police Department lacks equipment for such analyses."

This struck Massee as a glaring inadequacy so he asked Charles F. Rathbun, his personal attorney, to recommend a competent ballistics expert. Rathbun had spoken on the same program at a convention several months prior to the massacre with Major Calvin Hooker Goddard, the foremost ballistics expert in America. Rathbun suggested Goddard's name. No county funds were available for retaining Major Goddard whose fees were high, so Massee and Walter Olson, another member of the coroner's jury, furnished the money to bring Goddard to Chicago from New York where he was engaged in a private ballistics consulting business.[24]

Goddard was the star witness when Bundesen resumed the inquest into the massacre on April 13. The site of this session of the inquest, the eighth floor of the new State Street police headquarters, was jammed to capacity. In addition to Police Commissioner Russell and all fifty-five of the police captains, there were in attendance one judge, one assistant attorney general, the members of the jury, one assistant state's attorney, an assortment of city and county officials, and dozens of newspaper reporters and photographers.

Bundesen opened the proceedings, reading this statement:

Since September 17, 1923 when Jerry O'Connor was slain in the first gang war killing, there have been two hundred thirteen gang killings. In only one instance has there been a conviction, and that was in the case of Sam Vinci sentenced to twenty-six years in the penitentiary for slaying a witness at a coroner's inquest. Vinci accused the witness of having killed his brother in a gang feud. Since 1923 only nineteen men have been tried for gang murders."[25]

Bundesen asserted that the unsolved gang murders in Chicago proved one thing: old methods of criminal investigation needed to be replaced by new ones. "The science of forensic ballistics or scientific identification of bullets and firearms is of recent origin," explained Bundesen. "It is based on the discovery that no two revolver barrels (or barrels of any form of weapon) make the same scratches on a bullet. By submitting discharged bullets to a microscopic examination, you will find very minute and distinct lines or scratches on them," he said. "No two weapons cause the same scratches; fired bullets are like fingerprints."[26]

Following this brief description of ballistics, Bundesen discussed Goddard's work. "The silent witnesses Major Goddard is searching for will tell their story truthfully and cannot be intimidated or kidnapped," said Bundesen. "For the first time in the history of the city, modern scientific methods are being applied to solve crime."

The coroner explained that Goddard had examined not only the bullets fired in the massacre but also all police weapons in Chicago, Cicero, Melrose Park, and in the county highway police force. The scope of Goddard's inquiry included as many of the gang murders dating back to 1923 as there were guns or bullets available in the possession of the authorities. Goddard had been given forty-one weapons seized from notorious gangsters in the past, and he had been given bullets taken from the bodies of seventy-four of the gang war victims. According to Bundesen, Goddard had fired hundreds of test bullets from the weapons of the police and the gangsters, the firing being done mostly in the basement of Massee's home since, at this time, there was no crime lab in Chicago. Weapons were discharged into a large can filled with waste, and the bullets were recovered, imbedded in the waste.[27]

Major Goddard, a middle-aged man, with the voice and presence of a clergyman, then took center stage. Goddard fastened three murders upon George Maloney, a Chicago gangster and beer runner. He told how Maloney had been indicted for and had pleaded not guilty to the murders of two of the men, Hugh ("Stubby") McGovern and William ("Gunner") McPadden, who had been shot to death as they sat in the

Granady Cafe at 68th Street and Cottage Grove Avenue on December 31, 1928. Goddard told how Maloney had been caught at the scene with a revolver in his hand, but no one had seen him fire the weapon. Maloney denied having shot the two men. Telltale bullets found in the bodies of McGovern and McPadden and examined by Goddard matched exactly with test bullets fired from George Maloney's revolver.

"And there is more," said Goddard to his spellbound audience. "From studying the bullet which, in 1928, killed Thomas Johnson, south side gangster, I found that it, too, was fired from the Maloney weapon, and that the bullet in Johnson's body matches perfectly with the test bullet from Maloney's gun."

Goddard then focused on the massacre. "Evidence," he said, "establishes two facts. First, assassins wielded two machine guns and a rifle in killing the Moran hoodlums. Second, my examination of all Chicago, Cicero, Melrose Park, Chicago Heights, and other suburban police departments proves that the bullets found in the Moranites bodies' were *not* fired from police guns."

After Goddard's presentation, Assistant State's Attorney David Stansbury identified Fred ("Killer") Burke as one of assassins in the St. Valentine's Day Massacre.[28] Disclosure of Burke's name followed information furnished by a witness who, while driving his automobile up close to the killers' Cadillac on February 14, noticed that the driver in police uniform lacked an upper front tooth. Detectives checked all dentists' offices in Chicago, and at the office of Dr. Loyal Tacker, whose office was located at 2530 North Clark Street, four blocks from the Moran garage at 2122 North Clark Street, they learned a man answering the description of the killer minus a tooth had been a patient recently. Tacker, who extracted the tooth, positively identified a picture of Burke at the police department.[29] Chicago police knew that at the time of the massacre Burke was a fugitive under indictment in Ohio for bank robbery and murder. They also were familiar with his modus operandi in bank robberies, which was to wear a police uniform.[30]

Establishing a Crime Lab

At a special meeting of the coroner's jury on April 19, Calvin Goddard tried to sell jurors on the idea that Chicago needed a bureau for the identification of firearms. His voice quiet, his tone matter-of-fact, Goddard talked about the tracing of bullets and the necessity for having experts familiar with every type of firearm and every type of ammunition. He said a trained expert could take a look at the powder burns on a dead man's coat and tell what sort of ammunition was used.

The proposed gun bureau should be staffed, in Goddard's view, with men who knew how to use microscopes and cameras and instruments of precision. "The city needs men who know about handwriting and typewriting, and who can just about tell the height, weight, age, sex, speed and mental condition from a person's footprints," Goddard said. "You also need a highly trained toxicologist—someone who can analyze stains and determine if they are bloodstains and whether the blood is human or not; who can analyze soil residues; tell from the dust on a man's shoes whether he was in the part of Cook County he claimed to have been in."

Coroner Bundesen and the jury agreed that Chicago needed a crime prevention bureau. But instead of its being in the police department or the coroner's office, they believed a chair of ballistics should be founded at some university so it would be "free of political interference."[31]

Burt Massee supported Goddard's idea, but, like Bundesen, Massee was loath to seek any connection between the bureau and local government. Massee belonged to the Chicago Crime Commission, a private reform agency whose members abhorred Chicago Mayor William Hale ("Big Bill") Thompson and his political machine. Massee met with representatives of the University of Chicago and Northwestern University in May 1929 to determine whether either wanted a crime lab.

Colonel John Henry Wigmore, dean emeritus of Northwestern's Law School, became an early supporter of the concept of a crime lab. The colonel regarded the lab project as "one of the most meritorious things I have ever taken part in."[32] Wigmore greased the wheels for Northwestern's board of trustees to approve the lab's affiliation with Northwestern in June 1929. In selling Massee's proposal to Northwestern, Wigmore stressed that a crime lab was "a natural consequence of the development of modern science."[33] Writing to the university faculty committee that endorsed the proposal and passed it on to the board of trustees, Wigmore stated that "what science has done for other branches of civic and industrial achievement, it can and should do for the detection of crime."

In June 1929, Massee established the Laboratory Corporation, a private, nonprofit organization connected with Northwestern University.[34] Massee, the person most committed to the lab, became the corporation's first president. He hired Major Goddard as the lab's director and immediately dispatched him to Europe to inspect police laboratories there. Goddard's trip to Europe was necessary because, as Goddard put it, "We had no precedent to go upon—at least on this side of the water."[35] Goddard left in July and visited the police labs and medicolegal institutes that were maintained in connection with the police departments of London, Paris, Lyons, Berlin, Dresden, Brussels, Lausanne, Vienna, Budapest, Rome, Madrid, Bucharest, and Copenhagen. Returning in the middle of October, Goddard prepared a seventy-five-page report in which he stated: "Europe is two generations ahead of the U.S. in scientific police work, and when I say two generations I mean at least sixty years."

While Goddard was in Europe, Massee tried to secure subscriptions to finance the lab's projected budget of $60,000 for the first year. He made a brief start at raising this money but left Chicago in mid-July to sail his yacht to the West Indies.[36] Lowell Thomas, the famous radio commentator and world traveler, and Count Felix Von Luckner, a retired German naval officer, accompanied Massee on the trip, which lasted until September 1. A few days after his return to Chicago, Massee's father died, which diverted his attention away from the crime lab project.[37] Then the stock market crashed.

By the time Massee was free to canvass Chicago businessmen for money, economic conditions had worsened to the point where fund-raising was difficult. Samuel Insull, the utilities magnate, pledged $15,000, and a few other businessmen, such as Julius Rosenwald, the president of Sears, Roebuck and Company, also contributed money to the Laboratory Corporation. With the continuance of the Depression, however, it became nearly impossible to obtain money for the lab, so Massee paid Major Goddard's salary of $15,000, rent for the space occupied by the lab, and most of the other operating expenses for the first year.

Since there was no space in the existing buildings on the McKinlock campus of Northwestern—that university's downtown seat—for the lab and no funds available for the erection of a new building to house it, Massee leased quarters near the McKinlock campus at 155 East

Ohio Street. The lab's five thousand square feet of work space was consumed by laboratories, a museum, and a library. Although the lab did not formally open until February 1, 1930, Massee paid Goddard's salary in 1929 in order that the ballistics expert could develop plans for the lab and, at the same time, track down the perpetrators of the St. Valentine's Day Massacre.

"Killer" Burke

A breakthrough in the massacre case occurred in December when a police officer in St. Joseph, Michigan, tried to arrest two motorists who were involved in an auto collision. One of the motorists drew a .45-caliber automatic pistol and fired three shots, killing the policeman. The murderer escaped, using a passing motorist's car, but papers found in the murderer's wrecked automobile led to a search of his home in St. Joseph. There it was discovered that the man, who had been using the pseudonym of Frederick Dane, was Fred R. Burke, who Chicago police believed was the leader of the execution squad on February 14, 1929.

Upon entering Burke's home, police discovered Burke's woman companion, Viola Brenneman. She told police that after the Chicago massacre of seven gangsters Burke had promised his wife, whom he had since deserted, that he would never be taken alive by police for his part in the murders. Burke's woman companion said they were living together in Hammond, Indiana, the day of the massacre and that Burke left there at 7:30 A.M. that morning. The massacre occurred at 10:30 A.M. She told the police that Burke constantly talked about Al Capone.

On the second floor of Burke's St. Joseph house, under a carpet, police found a trapdoor that led to a room no detective would suspect existed in the house. This led to the roof where there was a flap through which one could emerge and drop to the outside of the house. A search of the bungalow revealed two Thompson machine guns, two high-powered rifles, a shotgun, seven automatic revolvers, eleven tear gas bombs, several bottles of nitroglycerin, and ammunition by the packs. Bonds valued at $319,850 were in his closet. Of these $112,000 worth had been taken in a bank robbery at Jefferson, Wisconsin, the previous month.

Deputy Police Commissioner John Stege and Pat Roche, chief investigator for State's Attorney Swanson, traveled to St. Joseph and questioned the woman who was known there as Mrs. Viola Dane, the wife of Fred Dane. Through an arrangement with Coroner Bundesen, the guns and bullets found in Burke's house were brought to Chicago where Calvin Goddard would conduct tests to determine if Burke's guns were used in the massacre. Law enforcement officials were all positive they had proved Burke to have been the leader of the Chicago execution squad, but they wanted Goddard to supply even more conclusive evidence. Stege and Roche said they had obtained information that the Moran gangsters were slain because of numerous hijackings of whiskey, probably from trucks going through Hammond. Burke and a man they believed was James Ray or Gus Winkler were hired to murder the Moran gang members. Burke, they said, achieved his reputation in 1927 when he allegedly killed Frankie Yale (or Uale), Sicilian boss of Brooklyn's gangsters. "Burke and his partner obtained the aid of two of Al Capone's truck drivers. The truck drivers were involved in the assassination plot because they could identify the hijackers and after they fingered the Moranites, their mission was done," said Roche. According to Stege, Burke and Ray, dressed as police officers, told the Moran boys to line up, faces to the wall, before executing them.[38]

Back in Chicago, Goddard fired bullets from Burke's guns into cotton waste, retrieved the bullets, and compared them with the bullets taken from the bodies of James Clark and Reinhardt Schwimmer, two of the victims of the massacre. Goddard's studies demonstrated that the two guns found in the Burke home had been used in the St. Valentine's Day Massacre. Goddard did not pin various of the fatal bullets to one particular gun but satisfied himself "by determining that the single bullet from the body of Reinhardt Schwimmer had been fired by one of the two guns and that one of the bullets from the body of James Clark had issued from the other."

That was not all. After obtaining the two machine guns found in Fred Burke's home, Goddard asked the New York Police Department to lend him the bullets taken from the corpse of Brooklyn gang leader Frankie Uale in July 1927. Goddard's tests showed that the fatal slugs that killed Uale were fired from one of the machine guns seized at the St. Joseph home of Fred Burke. In other words, Frank Uale (Yale) was murdered with one of the machine guns used in the St. Valentine's Day Massacre.[39]

Goddard's discovery provided a strange sequel to the massacre, one that demonstrated in a dramatic way the power of science when applied to crime fighting. A man is killed on a street in Brooklyn in 1927. One thousand miles away and months later, seven men are killed in a Chicago garage. Nearly a year passes, and a motorist shoots a patrolman in the little town of St. Joseph, Michigan. The most streetwise detective could not connect the three occurrences on the known facts. However, the scientist could peer through his microscope, read the markings on the shells and bullets, establish linkages between the events, and lay the groundwork for criminal prosecutions.

Deputy Commissioner Stege offered an explanation for the connection between those seemingly isolated events. He said that Uale was slain on the orders of Al Capone following Capone's discovery that Uale had been responsible for the hit on Capone's ally Tony Lombardo, who ruled the Unione Siciliana in Chicago. Soon after Lombardo's murder, Uale was killed in Brooklyn. Two pistols thrown away by Uale's slayers were traced to Parker Henderson of Miami, Florida, who said he got them from Al Capone. Both New York and Chicago police subscribed to the theory that Joe Aiello, who allied himself with the Moran gang, had induced Uale to send killers to Chicago to slay Lombardo and that Capone, in turn, had sent killers to New York to avenge Lombardo's death. Police officials also thought that Capone hired killers to carry out both the massacre and the Uale murder[40] and then sought shelter in prison in Pennsylvania to protect his own life.[41]

On December 23, Goddard presented the results of his tests to the Bundesen jury, which by now consisted of Colonel A. A. Sprague, who replaced Walter Olson of the original jury; Cyrus H. McCormick, who replaced Fred Berstein; Burt Massee; Master in Chancery Walter W. L. Meyer; Dean John V. McCormick of Loyola University Law School; and attorney Felix J. Streychmans.

Goddard showed that markings made first by the extractor, the firing pin, the rifling, and the ejector were the same on the bullets taken from the bodies and on the bullets fired in the tests. "The markings are as definite as fingerprints," Goddard said, "and are never alike on any two guns ever made."[42]

Based on Goddard's findings, the Bundesen jury recommended

"that the said Burke, now a fugitive from justice, be apprehended and held to the Grand Jury on the charge of murder as a participant in the murder of James Clark.[43]

Michigan authorities captured "Killer" Burke the following April but refused to surrender him to Illinois and instead tried him for the murder of the St. Joseph patrolman. Burke pleaded guilty to the charge of slaying a policeman, was sentenced to life in prison, and died there.[44]

The Crime Lab and Gangbusting

Approximately one year from the day "Killer" Burke crashed his car in St. Joseph, Michigan, the Scientific Crime Detection Laboratory officially opened. On that day, February 1, 1930, there was practically no interest anywhere else in the United States in applying science to solve crimes. No U.S. police departments maintained labs; none undertook any work to develop scientific methods of crime detection. Fingerprinting was the only available method even bordering on the scientific.[45]

Of course, the idea of crimefighters as scientists was already afoot in the twenties because of the police science movement. August Vollmer started the first academic department of police science in the United States at the University of California at Berkeley in 1908, and the notion of educating police officers spread across the country.

Employment of scientists at the Scientific Crime Detection Laboratory satisfied needs in two sectors of the criminal justice system, the police and the prosecutors. Examination and interpretation of physical evidence by laboratory staff members served a number of functions in the course of a criminal investigation conducted by the police:

1. Determining whether a crime had occurred
2. Identifying the person responsible for the crime
3. Eliminating from suspicion persons not associated with the crime
4. Providing information for directing the investigation
5. Reconstructing a criminal event[46]

Upon completion of a successful criminal investigation, the results of laboratory examinations assisted the prosecution in the preparation of a case. Subsequently, the evidence examiner served as an expert witness as the physical evidence was introduced at the trial.

A report of the lab's activities for the year 1930 suggests heavy concentrations of work in only a few areas. Of the 157 cases processed, 105 involved firearm examinations and 25 were "lie detector" examinations. Of the remaining cases, 10 were for fingerprints, 5 were document examinations, 2 cases each involved examinations of seminal stains, shoe prints, and tool marks, with the remaining 6 cases entailing some miscellaneous examinations. The caseload of the lab from December 1, 1930, to October 1, 1931, exceeded 200. In 1931, the full-time staff, including Goddard as director, was fourteen.[47]

While ostensibly the crime lab was founded to clear up Chicago's gang wars, scientists who worked there enjoyed only modest success in solving gang killings. Efforts by the scientists to find out the identities of the St. Valentine's Day killers continued, but no one was ever tried for the massacre. Insofar as organized crime was concerned, the symbolic effects of the lab were important. On account of brazen and brutal gang murders such as the St. Valentine's Day Massacre, "Chicago" in the 1920s became an internationally recognized code word for crime. The lab helped to restore the city's good name.[48] In addition, the crime lab's entry into the city's war against Capone instilled a "fear of the unknown" in the minds of gangsters.

The best example of this fear is an incident that took place some time in 1930. One day as Leonarde Keeler, the lab's lie-detector specialist, was alone in his private office, two tough-looking guys sauntered in and shut the door. When Leonarde asked "What can I do for you?" their eyes glared at him. One of them said, "We'll pay you $50,000 for the bullet that killed Jake Lingle." Leonarde stalled, lying that he did not know the combination to the safe. He said he'd have to get the combination from an assistant. "Wait here," Leonarde said. He walked out of his office and told each of his workers, "Go back to the shooting range. Start firing. Hurry!"

Returning to his office, Keeler found the two strangers waiting for him. He sat behind his desk and started to explain, "Sorry, gentlemen. I can't give you the bullet. It's evidence in a murder case."

As the men began to move toward Keeler, the building shook and the windows rattled from the roar of machine guns. Scared, the men hightailed it out of Leonarde's office and ran out to their getaway car.[49]

6

The Colonel, Jake, and Scarface Al

The murder of *Tribune* reporter Jake Lingle on June 9, 1930, energized the movement to get Capone. This event caused Colonel Robert R. McCormick, the owner of the *Tribune*, to join forces with Frank Loesch, Burt Massee, and Calvin Goddard.

A pedestrian tunnel under North Michigan Avenue near Grant Park provided the spot for the Lingle murder. Lingle passed through the subway, headed for the 1:30 P.M. Illinois Central train to the Washington Park racetrack at Homewood, Illinois, south of Chicago. His usual cigar was clenched between his teeth. A man nearly six feet tall walked up behind him, pulled a .38 from his pocket, lifted the weapon until the muzzle pointed at the back of Lingle's head, and pulled the trigger. After a bullet had crashed through the reporter's brain, Lingle fell dead with the lighted cigar still held between his teeth.[1]

The killer walked to the stairway leading out of the tunnel to the east side of Michigan Avenue and dashed out on North Michigan Avenue. Dodging traffic, he reached the northwest corner of Michigan and Randolph. A traffic policeman pursued the killer west on Randolph Street, then north through an alley, west to Wabash Avenue, and then south. When the policeman lost the slayer in a crowd, the chase ended.[2]

The Colonel Declares War

Colonel McCormick saw this killing as an attack on the *Tribune*. The Colonel, who in the military received the Distinguished Service Medal for "prompt action in battle," reacted to the Lingle murder as if he were still in combat in World War I.

Years later McCormick would recall the thoughts that ran through his mind the day Lingle was murdered:

I remembered that one should always reply to a sudden attack with an immediate counter-offensive. It seemed then that the choice was war or surrender, battle or the inevitable servitude of cowardice. I did not know the man who was killed, I had no idea of his private affairs, and practically no knowledge of his duties, but I had seen gangland rise from the murder of humble immigrants until it had reached the employee of a newspaper. If the battle was not waged here and now, it would be waged under less advantageous circumstances.[3]

Descending from his twenty-fourth-floor office in the Tribune Tower on March 9, McCormick marched into the fourth-floor newsroom and took command of the handling of the story of Lingle's murder. He ordered the posting of a $25,000 reward. The following morning the *Tribune* banner read: "OFFER $25,000 FOR ASSASSIN."

GUNMAN SLAYS ALFRED LINGLE IN I.C. SUBWAY
$25,000 for Capture is Tribune Offer

Alfred J. Lingle, better known to his world of newspaper work as Jake Lingle, and for the last eighteen years a reporter of the *Tribune* was shot to death yesterday in the Illinois Central subway at the east end of Michigan Boulevard at Randolph Street. The Tribune offers $25,000 as reward for information which will lead to the conviction of the slayer or slayers.[4]

The *Tribune* story recalled the 1926 murder of Don Mellett, a Canton, Ohio, editor shot by gangsters and commented that "these two are the only outstanding cases in which newspapermen paid with their lives for working against organized criminals."[5] The next paragraph mentioned that Lingle's was the twelfth gang slaying in Chicago in ten days. A couple of paragraphs later, the following was disclosed:

Because of his close friendship with Commissioner Russell and with other officials and leading politicians, Lingle was frequently besought by his hoodlum and racketeer acquaintances to use his influence to obtain concessions for them to pursue a profitable lawlessness. Invariably he told them that he could gain no such permission for them if he tried; that if they attempted to go ahead with their plans, they would surely be brought to answer before the law.[6]

A cartoon in the next day's *Tribune* showed "Chicago's Gangland" challenging law enforcement with a glove across the face. Following the lead of the front-page cartoon, the *Tribune* entitled its main editorial "The Challenge." After describing the killing, it said:

> The meaning of this murder is plain. It was committed in reprisal and in attempt at intimidating. Mr. Lingle was a police reporter and exceptionally well informed. His personal friendships included the highest police officials and the contacts of his work had made him familiar with most of the big and little fellows of gangland. What made him valuable to his newspaper marked him as dangerous to the killers.[7]

And the editorial concluded: "The *Tribune* accepts this challenge. It is war."[8]

Portrait of a Police Reporter

Born on the west side of Chicago in 1891, Jake Lingle obtained a job as a $12-a-week copyboy at the *Tribune* in 1912. He advanced to the job of "legman," never writing a news story. He would go to the crime scenes, collect information, and feed it to others to rewrite.[9]

Lingle knew persons from all walks of life in Chicago. Before the gangster era, the private detective agencies in Chicago were part of his beat. Thus, he had become well acquainted with the late William A. Pinkerton, William J. Burns, Raymond Burns, and other leaders in the private security field. When the United States entered World War I, Lingle enlisted and used his investigative knowledge in naval intelligence.

Lingle got to know the overlords of Chicago gangdom such as James ("Big Jim") Colosimo and later Johnny Torrio in the years between 1913 and 1919. He hung out with those men at Colosimo's restaurant on Wabash Avenue at 22nd Street, where some of the *Tribune*'s beat reporters, together with other newspaper workers, often gathered. Torrio at that time was an unknown hoodlum from the east side of New York, who attracted little attention.

For years Lingle developed friendships with members of the police department from the chief down. One of his closest pals in 1930 was

Chicago's chief of police, Bill Russell. Their friendship dated to twenty years before.[10] From Russell, Jake learned to feel at ease around police and criminals, and because of this trait, he developed an insider's knowledge of their lives and haunts.[11]

Lingle also counted among his friends the current governor of Illinois, its attorney general, and its first assistant attorney general. These government leaders knew what everyone else knew: Lingle listed Al Capone as his special friend.

Lingle first became acquainted with Capone when Torrio brought "Scarface Al" to Chicago. Lingle knew Capone when he was an inconspicuous figure and continued to associate with him as Capone grew in power. Capone granted Jake interviews, but theirs was more than a reporter-source relationship. As a token of how he felt about Jake, the gangster gave the reporter a $250 belt buckle, monogrammed in diamonds.

Lingle's family life centered around his wife, Helen, and their two children. Alfred, Jr., was six years old at the time of his father's murder, and Dolores was five. Jake had purchased a summer home at Long Beach, Indiana, on Lake Michigan. He paid $10,000 of its $16,000 price in cash.[12] On June 9, Helen Lingle was preparing to leave the next day with her two children for Long Beach. On June 10, she was planning her husband's funeral.

Lingle's funeral revealed that he was no ordinary legman. Thousands attended the ceremonies. Men and women squeezed into Our Lady of Sorrows Church on the west side and crowded the sidewalks and the streets outside. State's Attorney John A. Swanson, Coroner Herman N. Bundesen, County Judge Edmund K. Jareck, and Chief of Detectives John Stege attended the funeral. Pallbearers included Commissioner of Police Russell; First Assistant Attorney General Harry A. Ash; police Lieutenant Tom McFarland; and five of Lingle's newspaper associates.[13]

In life Lingle had pretended he was a wealthy reporter. When he died, his salary was $65 a week. But Lingle had talked to his buddies at the *Tribune* about inheritances from his deceased father and deceased uncle. Lingle told his associates that by pyramiding he had amassed a fortune in the stock market. Following the crash in 1929, Lingle told his friends that the collapse had wiped out his new fortune but left his original holdings intact.

Like others fascinated by easy money in the late twenties, Lingle was a big spender. He rode in a limousine, driven by a private chauffeur. At the racetracks, he sometimes bet $1,000 on a single race. Lingle always gave the impression that he was winning at the races, never mentioning when he lost. [14]

This was Jake Lingle as he was known before his murder. It was not the complete picture, as Colonel McCormick's investigation would prove.

McCormick's Investigation

Following Lingle's murder, a perplexing situation confronted the slain reporter's boss. On the one hand, Colonel McCormick vowed to catch and punish Lingle's killer. On the other hand, he felt he could not rely on the police or the state's attorney. Local law enforcement authorities had won only one gang murder case throughout Prohibition.

As president of the Chicago Newspaper Publishers' Association, McCormick called a meeting of the publishers, which was held in the afternoon after Lingle's funeral, on June 12. The colonel offered to pay the full expense of the investigation above what could be paid by the county. He proposed to place the case in the hands of two men, Charles F. Rathbun, as prosecutor, and Pat Roche, as chief investigator. Several publishers approved the plan; none opposed it. McCormick then talked with State's Attorney Swanson who accepted the offer of assistance.[15]

Swanson appointed Rathbun, a leading trial lawyer in Chicago, to the post of assistant state's attorney. Rathbun was a member of the law firm of Kirkland, Fleming, Green, and Martin, regular counsel for the *Tribune*, and a participant in many of the famous battles waged by the *Tribune* on behalf of freedom of the press. Rathbun had already been involved on the fringe of Chicago's private war against organized crime. Rathbun had recommended Calvin Goddard to Burt Massee when Massee was looking for a ballistics expert to examine cartridges and shells found at the scene of the St. Valentine's Day Massacre.

At the time of the Lingle murder, Pat Roche was already a member of the staff of State's Attorney Swanson. Roche had established himself as one of the top detectives of his day. His exploits as a patrolman in

Chicago and as an operative of the Special Intelligence Unit of the Treasury Department had earned him national recognition. According to Roche's peers, he was "swift to seize upon clues, to weigh their significance, and to match them into a pattern of proof."[16] Swanson assigned Roche to team up with Rathbun.

To coordinate the efforts of those involved in the Lingle case, State's Attorney Swanson called a conference in his office on June 19. Those present were the state's attorney, prosecutor Rathbun, investigator Roche, Coroner Bundesen, Commissioner Alcock, and John E. Norton, the chief of detectives. Swanson announced that Rathbun and Roche would direct all activities in the Lingle investigation, and he asked the other officials to present all evidence to that office. The state's attorney also urged that secrecy be maintained to prevent the leaking of clues. A big obstacle to solving the Lingle murder, he said, would be too much publicity. Swanson feared that newspapers, in their desire to compete with one another, might reveal inside information on what the investigators were planning to do and that publicizing the information would help the murderers evade authorities.[17]

Follow the Money

Once the inquiry began, prosecutor Rathbun uncovered evidence concerning Lingle's financial operations. Probate court records showed that the "fortune" left Lingle by his father was less than $500. The estate of his uncle was but $7,000, and of this Jake Lingle came into only $1,000. Lingle's winnings in the stock market were found to have been losses. He had never taken a profit. No records could be found of his racetrack wagers. While Rathbun investigated these matters, the *Tribune* became so flooded with rumors about Lingle that it ran this editorial:

> At the time of his death and for several days thereafter the general assumption was that he was killed to prevent the exposure in the *Tribune* of facts about gangland which were known to him.
> More recently rumors have arisen regarding Mr. Lingle's relations with gangdom. It has been said that he was, in one fashion or another, an ally and that he was killed for violating in some manner the code of gangdom.[18]

Ten days later State's Attorney Swanson issued a report, prepared by Rathbun, giving an detailed account of Lingle's finances. Rathbun's search had gone back two and a half years, to January 1, 1928. The slain reporter had maintained only one bank account, which was in the Lake Shore Trust and Savings Bank. Rathbun found that Lingle's bank deposits in 1928 were $26,500; in 1929, $25,100; and in 1930, $12,300—a total for the entire period of $63,900. Canceled checks drawn by Lingle for the thirty-month period revealed that they were cashed at racetracks and dog tracks and at the counter of the Lake Shore bank. Checks cashed at racetracks during the period totaled $15,000, those cashed at dog tracks totaled $2,600, and the counter checks totaled $15,470—showing total withdrawals of $33,070 from the $63,900 he had deposited. Rathbun was convinced that some of the deposits in the account represented racetrack winnings.[19]

Canceled checks indicated Lingle had drawn checks totaling $6,000, which he applied on the payment of his summer home at Long Beach, Indiana. One check was payable to a brokerage house, in the sum of $1,500. Of the rest of the canceled checks, one was a check for $500 issued to Daniel Gilbert, a police captain who commanded the central police district, downtown. Captain Gilbert explained that he had been telling Lingle about his financial troubles and that the reporter had insisted on lending him $500.[20]

In his stock market investments, Lingle could have sold his holdings at the height of the bull market in September 1929 and realized a profit of $85,000. But he hung on, until the crash wiped out the $85,000 profit and left him with a loss of $75,000. Lingle had lost over $52,000 and at the time of his death had owed his brokers an additional $22,000. Lingle had an interest in five brokerage accounts. The first was a joint account with Jackson Brothers, Boesel and Company, in which Lingle and Commissioner Russell were equally interested. In the period from November 26, 1928, when Lingle and Russell opened that account, until April 2, 1930, when Lingle made his last deposit in another account, he had deposited a total of $67,500 in all five accounts. That amount, however, did not represent gross additional income of Lingle. Records indicated that some of the funds deposited by Lingle in his stock accounts had come from his bank account, and vice versa.[21]

While Rathbun could not ascertain the net income of Lingle, it was large for a legman-reporter. How had he amassed so much money? To quote the Rathbun report:

> As to the source of the moneys put up by Lingle in these stock accounts and deposited by him in his bank account, we have thus far been able to come to no conclusion except as indicated in the accounts. There have been many rumors as to where he obtained these moneys, but no man has ever been successfully prosecuted on a rumor alone, nor has the solution of any crime been reached by hastily giving credit to rumors.[22]

Tracing the Murder Weapon

Calvin Goddard, director of Northwestern's crime lab, supplied the first good lead in the Lingle investigation. Goddard restored the serial number that had been filed off the .38-calibre weapon used to kill Lingle. Goddard passed this information on to Coroner Bundesen who telephoned the Colt factory in Connecticut to give Colt officials the number of the weapon.

Within an hour, Bundesen received a telegram that the gun had been sold in June 1928, with five others of the same make, to Peter Von Frantzius, a sporting goods dealer on the north side of Chicago. Von Frantzius had supplied the weapons for the St. Valentine's Day Massacre in 1929. Von Frantzius admitted that north side hoodlum Frank Foster had bought all six guns.[23]

On June 20 Rathbun and Roche got a tip that Frank Foster might be in Los Angeles. Three detectives from Roche's staff took the first train for Los Angeles, and thus came one of the first proofs that without special private sponsorship the Lingle inquiry could not have made much headway. The state's attorney had no money with which to send detectives to the Pacific Coast, but the *Tribune* provided the necessary funds. Detectives from Roche's staff arrested Foster in Los Angeles on July 1, 1930, but Foster declined to come to Chicago voluntarily.

Back in Chicago, Rathbun secured Foster's murder indictment to facilitate extradition. On July 16, California authorities placed Foster on a train bound for Chicago. At a point several miles from the downtown Chicago terminal, Rathbun's men removed Foster from the train and drove him to a Loop hotel, where Rathbun held Foster incommunicado and questioned him.

Foster refused to disclose what had become of the weapon Von Frantzius had sold him, and eventually he was placed in the county jail where he stayed until his trial began on November 29, 1930. A judge continued Foster's case several times, and finally, on June 19, the judge granted the prosecution's nolle prosse motion in the criminal court, thus dismissing the case. Chief Investigator Roche announced at the time that the evidence against Foster was insufficient.[24]

Newspaper War

Important events preceded the state's dropping of charges against Foster. One of them was a newspaper war. Unity prevailed when the newspaper publishers of Chicago met on June 11 to consider the crime situation in Chicago. The men unanimously adopted the following resolution:

> The intolerable outrages of the last year against civic decency and public security in Chicago have culminated dramatically in the cowardly murder of Alfred J. Lingle, a newspaper reporter.
> The undersigned Chicago daily newspapers interpret that murder as an especially significant challenge to the millions of decent citizens who have suffered the vicious activities, in defiance of law and order, of some paltry hundreds of criminal vagrants known as gangsters.
> Considering the causes and the connotations of the unbelievable total of one hundred gang murders in little more than a year and acting in accord and unison we pledge our resources to the cleanup of gang, police, official, and any other public viciousness wherever it may appear in order that corruption and the resulting gang activities may be brought to an end and thereby restoring to the citizens of Chicago civic decency and security of life and property.[25]

This resolution was signed by representatives of the *Daily Illustrated Times*, the *Daily News*, the *Evening American*, the *Evening Post*, the *Herald and Examiner*, the *Journal of Commerce*, and the *Tribune*. Colonel McCormick, the publisher of the *Tribune*, outlined his plan to put Charles F. Rathbun and Pat Roche in charge of the Lingle investigation. His colleagues approved. Representatives of the newspapers further agreed that when news arose during the inquiry, Rathbun and Roche should not show favoritism toward the *Tribune* in its release.

Furthermore, they concurred that murder clues would not be exposed in the daily press.

For a while the investigation went along without interference from the newspapers. Then, on June 21, the *Herald and Examiner* violated the publishers' pact, running a front-page story stating that the murder weapon had been identified, that it had been sold by Von Frantzius to Frank Foster, and that the state's attorney was pursuing Foster.[26] The night before the story was printed, Roche's detectives had boarded a train for Los Angeles to arrest Foster. The story that Foster was being sought was published in the Hearst *Los Angeles Examiner* thirty-six hours before the detectives arrived in that city on their mission.[27]

The next day the *Herald and Examiner* printed a story disclosing that Roche was looking for "Red" Forsythe as the man who killed Lingle and that he also was hunting for two other men as Forsythe's accomplices.[28] Great care had been taken to keep these three men from knowing that they were being sought, but the *Herald and Examiner*'s story ruined any chance of nabbing the suspects. Following the lead of the *Herald and Examiner*, other Chicago newspapers published information relating to the Lingle inquiry. Some newspapers printed rumors. Reporters from newspapers whose publishers had signed the resolution on June 11 spied on Rathbun. Editorial writers from rival newspapers labeled Lingle a racketeer, fixer, and gangster.

Realizing the Lingle case had captured the nation's interest, editors of newspapers in other cities sent staff reporters to Chicago. Harry T. Brundidge, a reporter of the *St. Louis Star* visited the *Tribune* office and the offices of the other newspapers and probed into the newspaper war in Chicago.

In his first story on the subject, which later was printed in the *Tribune*, Brundidge zeroed in on the murder of Julius Rosenheim, a stool pigeon who was killed on February 1, 1930. Calling Rosenheim "the Squawker," Brundidge revealed that Rosenheim had ties with a reporter for the *Chicago Daily News* who used Rosenheim as a stoolie. According to Brundidge, "the Squawker," like Lingle, lived like a king, driving a very expensive car and buying stylish things. The truth, in Brundidge's view, was that Rosenheim was a "shakedown artist" who forced gamblers, brothel keepers, booze and beer barons, and other racketeers to pay him money under threat of exposure in the *News*. Rosenheim could make good on his threats because his job, like Lingle's, was to supply a reporter with inside "scoops" on gangdom.[29]

In a second article Brundidge charged that newspapermen on other Chicago papers were "racketeers."[30] Part of his story consisted of an interview with the publisher of the *Tribune* in which Colonel McCormick was quoted as saying that he would ask the grand jury to investigate charges against newspapermen. Brundidge stated that whereas Lingle had been nicknamed the "unofficial chief of police of Chicago," another reporter was known as the "unofficial mayor of Chicago." As a solution to the problem of an alleged alliance between the newspapers and the gangs, Brundidge advocated a grand jury investigation of connections between various reporters and Al Capone.[31]

Reacting to Brundidge, Colonel McCormick addressed this letter to State's Attorney Swanson:

> Dear Mr. Swanson:
>
> When Lingle was murdered four weeks ago I offered assistance to the prosecution by putting at your disposal Mr. Charles Rathbun, an experienced lawyer, whom you formerly honored with the offer of a permanent appointment in your office. This offer you accepted and under your direction Mr. Rathbun has organized and carried on an investigation. We have given him every assistance in our power and through the endorsements on the pay checks of Lingle found where he had been banking and with the public spirited cooperation of the bank secured details of this bank accounts which may furnish the clew which will capture his murderer and may furnish avenues into the gangland jungle.
>
> It is natural that during such investigation a multitude of rumors should have arisen, many of them highly imaginative, it would seem, but some of them very definite and strongly supported. In fact, the names of certain newspaper officials have been bandied around until they are popularly accepted as guilty.
>
> It seems to me in justice to these men full investigation should be made to establish the innocent and the guilty and also to free from the entire profession the stigma which has been created by the wide dissemination of rumors of all kinds.
>
> In addition to the official investigators there have been a number of amateurs at work, among them Mr. Harry T. Brundidge, a writer for the *St. Louis Star*, who asserts that he has unearthed much incriminating evidence. He has written two stories for his

newspaper, the *St. Louis Star,* which have been reproduced in the *Chicago Tribune.*

The revelations of the last two weeks have been distressing to many of us. We wish the matters exposed had never occurred. We tend to wish that soiled linen be not washed in public, but out of so much evil a greater good may come. The activities of Lingle and men of his tripe are like paths leading into the forest of crime which hitherto has proven trackless. By following them, the whole criminal organization which has Chicago by its throat may be surrounded and destroyed.

Therefore, it is my opinion that Mr. Brundidge should be interrogated and that all probable clues disclosed by him should be mercilessly followed up regardless of where they lead. To do this work will demand a larger personnel than now engaged. It is not within the capacity of Mr. Rathbun to increase his activities without diverting himself from his principal duty, the discovery of the circumstances of Mr. Lingle's murder and of the persons guilty of that crime.

I therefore suggest that further examination into the rumors aroused by this case be carried on by your regular staff or by special counsel competent to make such investigation.

Sincerely yours,
Robert F. McCormick[32]

Meanwhile, newspapermen at DeKalb, Illinois, found out that Leland Reese, the gangland reporter for the *Daily News* who had used Rosenheim as a paid informant, was severely injured in an automobile accident. The *Daily News* published on its front page a story by Reese, in which he told of being pursued by gangsters and then "sideswiped" and run off the road into a ditch.[33] Reese claimed that gangsters had threatened him with death, and for this reason the *Daily News* had supplied him with two bodyguards. In this story Reese gave the following information about the murder of Rosenheim: "I have been told by men who ought to know that he was killed in an effort to frighten the *Daily News* away from its attack on the Capone beer racket in the loop."

On July 11 the *Daily News* published a front-page story revealing that the heads of two private crime-fighting groups—Frank J. Loesch of the Chicago Crime Commission and Robert Isham Randolph of the Secret Six—had signed a letter sent to State's Attorney Swanson calling for the removal of Rathbun from the Lingle investigation.[34] After the story appeared, however, both Loesch and Randolph denied wanting to get rid of Rathbun.[35]

A Midnight Visit with Capone

Having stirred up trouble in Chicago, Harry Brundidge went to see the man he regarded as the best source of information on the Lingle killing. "Scarface Al" was in Florida, where he had been lying low ever since his release from prison on March 16, 1930. After a hot forty-eight-hour trip from St. Louis to Miami on July 17, Harry Brundidge got off the train at 8:15 P.M. Going directly to the Pancoast Hotel on the beach, Brundidge hired an automobile and drove to Capone's Palm Island residence. A guard stood at the iron gates and said Capone was out with his attorneys. "When will he return?" asked Brundidge. The guard shrugged and the writer sat down on the grass to wait. At 10 P.M. a big limousine arrived with Capone's younger brother, and a few minutes later another black sedan pulled up at the gates. Capone, with two armed guards and another man, stepped out, whereupon the reporter introduced himself.

"This is a surprise," said Capone. "Come on in."

A moment later Capone and Brundidge were seated on a divan on the sun porch of Capone's Palm Island home.

"You seem to have raised merry hell in Chicago," Capone began. "What brings you here?"

"I thought I would ask you who killed Lingle?"

"Why ask me?" he responded. Then, after a pause, he said in tones that carried conviction: "The Chicago police know who killed him."

The writer asked: "Was Jake your friend?"

"Yes, up to the day he died."

"Did you have a row with him?"

"Absolutely not."

"It is said you fell out with him because he failed to split profits from handbooks."

"Bunk. The handbook racket hasn't been really organized in Chicago for more than two years and any one who says it is doesn't know Chicago."

"If you did not have a row with Lingle, why did you refuse to see him upon your release from the workhouse in Philadelphia?"

"Who said I didn't see him?"

"The Chicago newspapers, the files of which, including his own paper, the *Trib*, set forth the fact."

"Well, if Jake failed to say I saw him—then I didn't see him."

"What about Jake's diamond belt buckle?"

"I gave it to him."

"Do you mind stating what it cost?"

"Two hundred fifty dollars."

"Why did you give it to him?"

"He was my friend."

"How many rackets was he engaged in?"

Capone shrugged his shoulders.

"What was the matter with Lingle, the horse races? How many other Lingles are there in Chicago in the newspaper racket?"

"Phooey, don't ask."

"Seriously, what do you think of newspaper men who turn their profession into a racket?"

"I think this: Newspapers and newspaper men should be busy suppressing rackets and not supporting them. It does not become me of all persons to say that, but I believe it."

"How many newspaper men have you had on your payroll?"

Again a pause punctuated the conversation. Capone shrugged and said: "Plenty."

"Have you had any telephone calls from newspaper men in Chicago since publication in the *St. Louis Star* that Lingle was not the only one in his profession in Chicago with a racket?"

"Plenty."

The big beer baron leaned over, put his left arm around Brundidge's shoulders, squeezed him, and said: "Listen, Harry: I like your face. Let me give you a hot tip. Lay off Chicago and the money hungry reporters. You're right; because you're right, you're wrong. You can't buck it, not even with the backing of your newspaper, because it is too big a proposition. No one man will ever realize just how big it is, so lay off."

"You mean?"

"I mean they'll make a monkey out of you before you get through.

No matter what dope you have to give that grand jury, the boys will prove you're a liar and a faker. You'll get a trimming."

"I'm going to quote you as saying that."

"If you do, I'll deny it."

Capone took Brundidge on a walk around the grounds surrounding his villa. Brundidge saw Capone's swimming pool and bathhouse, as fine as anything in Hollywood—the private pier, boathouse, high-powered speedboat, and palatial cruiser. As the two strolled along, the beams of a tropical moon danced on the waters of Biscayne Bay lighting up Capone's rock garden, fernery, and gorgeous trees and flowers.

"Are you afraid?" the writer asked.

"Of what? I go everywhere alone most of the time and would be happy here if the Miami police would let me alone. A little clique in Miami has tried to run me out of town, but I refuse to be chased. They have arrested me repeatedly, tried me unsuccessfully on a trumped up perjury charge and tried to padlock my home as a public nuisance because I kept a drink here for myself, as who in Miami doesn't? No, I'm not afraid. No harm will come to me, because I am out of all rackets. I will make Miami my home and will go to Chicago only occasionally. I had my success, saved my money, and now I'm through with the rackets."

"You certainly organized Chicago in a hurry," Brundidge said.

"Organized Chicago? Bah! How could any one man organize a city of 3,000,000? I was successful in some rackets up there, but to say that I organized the town is to be foolish."

"Let's quit talking about the rackets. You've seen the grounds. Now, how about a tour of my home?" Capone asked.

Of course, Brundidge said he would, so they walked through all seventeen rooms, from the bedrooms to the kitchen, where a fine catch of bonito (a species of mackerel), taken that same day was on ice. Capone told with pride how his hand and brain alone directed the decorators of his home. Following the tour of the house at one o'clock in the morning, Capone walked Brundidge to the front gate where a sedan was waiting. One of Capone's men drove the writer back to his hotel and talked with him there far into the night.[36]

Upon Brundidge's return to St. Louis, State's Attorney Swanson invited the St. Louis reporter to appear for questioning by his assistants. Brundidge declined the offer but did testify before the grand jury. The grand jurors then summoned a host of newspaper reporters, editors, and publishers. Those accused were called, and so were Colonel McCormick, publisher of the *Tribune*; Robert M. Lee, city editor of the *Tribune*; Walter Strong, publisher of the *Daily News*; and others. The jurors also called Captain William Russell and Corporation Counsel Ettelson, hoping to learn from them the manner of Russell's appointment as police commissioner. Rumor had it that the *Tribune* had dictated Russell's appointment to Mayor Thompson. Finally, the grand jury returned a report at the end of July to the chief justice of the criminal court. The jury discussed its inability to substantiate the evidence given by Brundidge, stating that most of Brundidge's testimony was hearsay. Then the report said:

> Numerous rumors appeared in the public press relative to the manner in which Russell was appointed commissioner of police. On the evidence that was produced for the grand jury by various public officials it is our opinion that his appointment came through the regular channels of the present city administration. Further, the grand jury recommends that the citizens of Chicago cooperate with the state's attorney's office and other law enforcing bodies, also with the special state's attorneys, Charles F. Rathbun and James E. McShane, and the investigators headed by Patrick T. Roche, chief investigator for the state's attorney's office, who are working solely on the Lingle murder, which we have every reason to believe will soon be solved.[37]

Turning on the "Heat"

Was the investigation failing? McCormick's band of privately sponsored prosecutors and detectives reviewed their work in October 1930. In a desperate move, Rathbun decided to put "heat" on the Capone gang. His idea was to "break up the joints that brought money to the gang."[38]

In the weeks that followed, bawdy houses, gambling dens, booze joints—the sources of gang income—were raided and closed; paraphernalia was seized; and the inmates, keepers, and operators were put in cells. Cicero, Capone's refuge, was invaded. Raiders, led by Rathbun and Roche, stormed Cicero hotels that were known as Capone hangouts. Running roughshod through the halls, detectives took passkeys and entered the rooms, collecting hoodlums, their women, guns, booze, and property.[39]

Capone wanted the raids to end so he sent a wealthy businessman to the offices of the investigators of the Lingle murder case. The businessman told Rathbun and Roche: "The 'Big Fellow' wants to see you."[40]

Late at night on October 21 a representative of Rathbun and Roche, known as Operative Number One, met with Al Capone at a suburban home.

"Here's what I want to tell you, and I won't be long about it," said Capone. "I can't stand the gaff of these raids and pinches. If it's going to keep up, I'll have to pack up and get out of Chicago."

Operative Number One replied: "The gaff is on for keeps. This town has been burning up since Jake Lingle was murdered."

"Well, I didn't kill Jake Lingle, did I?"

"We don't know who killed him."

"Why didn't you ask me? Maybe I can find out for you."

"Maybe you can."

"I don't know what the fellow who killed Jake looks like. I know none of my fellows did it. I like Lingle, and certainly I didn't have any reason to kill him."

Operative Number One described the killer, and then Capone supplied a motive for Lingle's murder.

"I have heard," said Capone, "that Lingle was involved in the attempts of the North Side gangsters to open a dog track in the Stadium."

Capone was referring to the fact that up to a month before the murder of Lingle the Capone gang had been operating two dog racetracks, one in Cicero, the other in Thornton. The north side gang had operated the Fairview dog track, but it had burned to the ground. Then the north side gang tried to establish an indoor dog racetrack in the Chicago Stadium.

"The North Side gang paid Lingle $30,000 to see to it that the police and the state's attorney would not bother them," explained Capone. "When Pat Roche and State's Attorney Swanson refused to allow anyone to operate a dog track at the Stadium, the gang blamed Lingle, and that's why Lingle was pushed [killed]."

Capone claimed that he didn't know the identity of the north siders who did the job and promised to find out. He told Operative Number One that when he obtained information on who killed Lingle he would send the same wealthy businessman to the operative. The operative was then driven away from the meeting place in Capone's automobile.[41]

Rathbun continued the raids on the dens of the Capone gang, causing Capone's representative in early November to request another meeting with Operative Number One. When the two got together, the Capone agent said, "Al wants to know if you will take the Lingle killer dead?"[42]

Operative Number One notified the Capone representative that the killer had to be taken alive. Furthermore, there would be no more meetings. What the Rathbun-Roche operative didn't tell Capone's agent was that the federal government possessed information suggesting a motive Capone himself might have had to kill Jake Lingle. Within three days after the reporter's murder, Justice Department officials had come to the *Tribune*, asking whether or not the *Tribune* had any knowledge of evidence concerning Capone's income. The investigators were looking for evidence upon which to base an indictment of Capone for income tax fraud and hoped for the newspaper's assistance. Although the *Tribune* knew of no evidence concerning Capone's sources of income, Lingle, through his in-depth knowledge of the gangster, might have known how Capone concealed the sources of his illegal profits. A dead man could not provide evidence to tax authorities.[43]

The Capture of Leo Brothers

The trail to Lingle's killer was cold, so Rathbun and Roche decided to "set a gangster to catch a gangster." They sent a man into the gangs and had him stay inside until he knew who killed Lingle. Secret agent John Hagen, an ex-con, identified a lamster from a St. Louis murder as a key suspect. First, Hagen got the name "Buster," then Bader.

From wiretaps of gangsters' phones, Rathbun and Roche found out that Bader lived at the Lake Crest Drive Apartment Hotel, 4827 Lake Park Avenue, in Chicago.[44] By a stroke of luck, Pat Roche knew a Rose Huebsch who lived at 4827 Lake Park Avenue, the same address as

"Bader." Huebsch's apartment was directly opposite Bader's, with a hallway between them.

Three men accompanied Roche to Huebsch's apartment, while Rathbun and several other men positioned themselves at the front and rear of the building and beneath Bader's window. Once inside Huebsch's apartment, Roche had Huebsch call the telephone number of the apartment building at ten o'clock at night. She asked the clerk to summon "Bader." The clerk rang Bader's house phone (which could not directly receive calls) and informed him there was a call in the lobby. When Bader left his apartment to go to the lobby, Roche pinned Bader against the wall in the hallway, while two of his assistants patted down the suspect.

The private law enforcers took Bader to a downtown hotel for interrogation, during which he admitted that his real name was Leo Vincent Brothers.[45] Witnesses were brought to the hotel suite, which served as the secret jail for Brothers. After eight witnesses had identified Brothers as the murderer of Lingle, Roche and Rathbun announced the capture of Brothers to the press.

Reporters delved into Brothers's background and came up with this biographical sketch: born April 14, 1899, in Belleville, Illinois; dropped out of school in the seventh grade; served in the Navy during World War I; married a young St. Louis girl; accused by St. Louis authorities of murder, robbery, arson, and bombing.[46]

Avenging the Murder of Lingle

Brothers's defense was to condemn those who accused him. Lawyers for the defendant received aid from some newspapers in Chicago that sought to hinder the prosecution of a murderer who had been stalked and apprehended by an agency set up and paid for by the *Tribune*. The defense cried persecution, and rival newspapers echoed the charge—that Colonel McCormick had spent thousands of dollars to pin the guilt for the murder of Lingle upon an innocent man.[47]

Realizing the defense's strategy was to try McCormick, the *Tribune*, or himself, Rathbun put Assistant State's Attorney C. Wayland Brooks in charge of the prosecution. When the trial of Leo Brothers for the murder of Alfred Lingle opened on March 16, 1931, the state produced eight witnesses to accuse Brothers. Next, the prosecution called an expert witness from the Scientific Crime Detection Laboratory, who identified the weapon that had killed Lingle and described how scientists had etched in with acids the mutilated numbers on the weapon by which it had been identified as having been sold to Frank Foster. Calvin Goddard, crime lab director, then testified that he had fired a test bullet from the weapon in evidence and, upon comparing it under a special microscope with the bullet taken from Lingle's head, had found the identifying marks on both bullets to be the same. Goddard stated that the bullet that killed Lingle had been fired from the weapon introduced by the prosecution in court.

Testimony by crime lab experts proved critical because no state witness had been able to testify that he saw Brothers fire the shot that killed Lingle. But one of the state's witnesses had testified that he saw Brothers drop the gun, the same weapon then before the court, and since Goddard had shown that this was the murder weapon, it followed that Brothers must have fired the shot.[48]

The defense called eight witnesses. Seven testified that the defendant was not the man who fled from the scene of the Lingle killing. The defense's main strategies were showing that the prosecution had failed to provide any motive and putting the *Tribune* on trial. "The great question here," shouted one of Brothers's attorneys during his closing argument, "is who killed Jake Lingle and why? Find the motive of this prosecution. Is it a prosecution by the state's attorney or by the *Chicago Tribune*?"

The verdict came after twenty-seven hours of deliberating: "guilty," with the sentence set at fourteen years.[49] Colonel McCormick endorsed the verdict. On June 9, 1931, one year to the day after Jake Lingle was murdered, McCormick paid to John Hagen the $25,000 that had been offered a year before. In announcing the payment of the reward, the *Tribune* praised Hagen for his courage and loyalty.[50] Thus, the murder of Lingle was avenged, with the private investigation and private prosecution of that crime dragging "Scarface Al" Capone a step closer to his own demise as a gang leader.

7

Labeling Capone

During the post-Pennsylvania prison phase of Al Capone's career, Henry Barrett Chamberlin, the operating director of the Chicago Crime Commission, cast Al Capone in the role of arch-villain in a miscellany of plots, schemes, and rackets. He accused Capone of all sinister activities with underworld origins. Chamberlin's accusations contained some truth, some hysteria, and some politics.

Two examples illustrate this point. First, Chamberlin believed that Capone was maneuvering to establish himself as the czar of organized labor. Capone dominated the plumbers' union, the street sweepers' union, the newsboys' union, the city hall clerks' union, and the marble setters' union. Chamberlin wondered which unions would be taken over next. He was certain that businessmen who had to work out union contracts with Capone would be worse off than countries forced to negotiate peace with Mussolini.

Second, Chamberlin became convinced that Capone was building a political machine and seeking to take city hall patronage from aldermen and members of the mayor's cabinet. Capone, it was thought, was back of a proposal to appoint his henchman, City Sealer Daniel A. Serritella, superintendent of streets—thus giving Capone control of an annual budget of $7,000,000, 3,000 jobs, and the supervision of $5,000,000 a year in street repair work.[1]

Responding to these indications that Capone was seeking to tighten his grip over the city's political and economic institutions, Chamberlin issued a blast proclaiming Capone and twenty-seven lesser gangsters "public enemies." On April 24, 1930, Chamberlin demanded that Police Commissioner William Russell "harass gangsters in every way; raid their whorehouses, gambling joints, night clubs and dog tracks."[2]

Chamberlin told Russell to acquire confidential information on the twenty-eight gangsters' political affiliations, business and residential addresses, banking connections, and financial interests.

Handling all the work for this negative publicity blitz that targeted gangsters, Chamberlin drafted a press release demanding that the twenty-eight be subjected to "vigilant watchfulness and arrest with appropriate court action whenever and as often as possible." In the same release, Chamberlin asked authorities to deport those who were criminal aliens and to prosecute those who had failed to pay their income taxes.[3] Chamberlin vowed to keep the light of publicity on Chicago's most infamous gangsters to the end that they were under the constant observance of law enforcement authorities.

"Public Enemies"

In offering the list of twenty-eight to the press, Chamberlin casually called them "public enemies" to *Tribune* reporter James Doherty. He never dreamed that the phrase "public enemies" would gain instant popularity. Doherty's story on the list, appearing in the evening edition on April 24, started with the statement that the Crime Commission had labeled twenty-eight of Chicago's best-known hoodlums as "public enemies" and had asked the police department "to treat them accordingly." The eight-column front-page headline in the *Tribune* was "LIST 28 AS PUBLIC ENEMIES." The gangsters were listed alphabetically, as follows:

Joe Aiello, once partner of Tony Lombardo in rulership of the Sicilian gang, and suspected of having instigated the murder of Lombardo. He was suspected of several other murders.

George "Red" Barker, served terms in two penitentiaries for robbery and was a defendant in a murder trial. Barker took command of the coal teamsters union through gun play and threats and controlled a string of unions.

James Belcastro, called "King of the Bombers" because he was the leader of Scarface Al's squad of bombers, involved in west side outlawry and known as a dangerous man.

Alphonse Capone, most notorious of the gangsters, head of a liquor, vice, and gambling syndicate, who was reported to have been seizing control of labor unions in order to gain more political power and wealth.

Ralph Capone, brother of Alphonse, was on trial in federal court on charges of income tax falsification.

Frank Diamond, west side Capone lieutenant, whose name had been mentioned in connection with several murders.

Terry Druggan, one of the Druggan-Lake team which made a fortune in beer, who would be charged with income tax evasion.

Rocco Fanelli, west side procurer and gunman, who, with others, sought to take control of west side vice for Capone's syndicate in 1927.

Joseph Genaro, an alcohol dealer and gunman from the south side Genaro clan, who was shot and named his assailants, but refused to aid in their prosecution when he recovered.

Jack Guzick [Jake Guzik], south side brothel keeper, saloon keeper, and Capone representative.

Frank Lake, the other half of the Druggan-Lake combination.

Lawrence Mangano, known as "Dago," the proprietor of the Minerva Athletic Club, which has been raided scores of times as a gambling joint.

Frank McErlane, an old-time criminal and bootlegger. Acquitted of two murders and accused of many others. Reputed to be the most violent criminal in Chicago.

Vincent McErlane, brother of Frank.

Jack McGurn, known as "Machine Gun" Jack, indicted as one of the participants in the Valentine Massacre and charged with many other shootings.

Leo Mongoven, bodyguard of Bugs Moran, who was under indictment for attempted extortion. He had been arrested many times.

George "Bugs" Moran, former convict, leader of the north side gang after the killing of Dion O'Banion, Earl "Hymie" Weiss and Vincent Schemer Drucci. He made peace with the Capone gang following the killing of seven members of his gang in the St. Valentine's Day massacre.

William Niemoth, member of the Saltis gang, wanted in Baltimore for a bank robbery and involved in many other big robberies.

Edward "Spike" O'Donnell, one-time politician, who was convicted of bank robbery. Later, he became a south side beer gang member who was involved in beer wars.

Myles O'Donnell, a member of west side O'Donnell's beer gang, tried and acquitted of the murder of one man, and accused of killing two other men.

William "Klondike" O'Donnell, boss of the O'Donnell clan and brother of Myles. He served one term in Leavenworth for a booze robbery.

Frank Rio, alias Cline, gunman and bodyguard for Capone. He served a year in a Pennsylvania prison with Capone for gun toting.

Joe Saltis, boss of southwest side beer territory, who acquired considerable wealth in the bootlegging business and was named in connection with many killings. He was acquitted of murdering one man.

James "Fur" Sammons, once sentenced to death for murder, served twenty years of a life sentence, only to be sent to federal prison for eighteen months for a booze robbery.

Danny Stanton, south side bootlegger, named in many murders but convicted of none, who joined the Capone gang and was said to have been doing Capone's bidding in labor union matters.

Tony "Mops" Volpe, a Capone right hand man.

William "Three Finger Jack" White, one-time safe blower, who became business agent of one of the branches of the teamsters union.

Jack Zuta, boss of the white slave traffic of the Middle West.[4]

Even though Capone wasn't listed first, thereafter people everywhere branded him "Public Enemy Number One." The phrase was picked up and used all over the world; a moviemaker even adopted it for a title of a film. Some time later, in a speech at a press veterans' dinner, Chamberlin said his concern at the time was in stirring up the police to do something about the twenty-eight men and there was no special significance to the words "public enemies." What popularized the label, according to Chamberlin, was the way reporters had "played up" the story.[5]

The Crime Commission Versus Capone

Chicago's underworld immediately felt the impact of Chamberlin's program. Within gangland circles Capone and others on the list were called "heat boys." Henry Barrett Chamberlin manipulated the media so the heat boys remained a focal point of attention. The operating director convinced the *Tribune* to publish mug shots of all twenty-eight enemies and planted the idea among newspaper reporters of adding the line "He is one of those named by the commission as a public enemy" whenever they referred to one of the twenty-eight in a story.[6] He even used the press as an unpaid medium for spreading propaganda about Public Enemy Number One, as the following excerpt from one of Chamberlin's talks on Chicago radio station WBBM shows:

> Capone is the most dangerous, the most resourceful, the most cruel, the most menacing, the most conscienceless of any criminal of modern times. He has contributed more to besmirch the fair name of Chicago than any man living or dead. . . . Beginning as a little ruffian in Brooklyn, by stages, through pandering, traffic in women, and murder, he has reached a place never before occupied by any of his kind in this country. His ruthlessness has frightened his enemies. His employment of legal counsel, who ought to be ashamed of their employment, has enabled him to take advantage of the technicalities of the law. His bribery and debauchery of those charged with the administration of criminal justice has been effective. . . . But this lone gorilla of gangland is being cornered. . . . The end is certain, his notoriety, for a time the secret of his strength, promises to be the instrument of his undoing.[7]

To disseminate negative publicity, Chamberlin deployed another weapon in his arsenal, the Commission's journal *Criminal Justice*. As the editor of *Criminal Justice*, Chamberlin ran the cartoons of John T. McCutcheon and Carey G. Orr of the *Chicago Tribune*. He selected cartoons with an eye toward increasing the pressure on public officials to take action against the public enemies and rallying businessmen to join the Commission's crime drive. One cartoon, for example, showed a police officer tied to a criminal near a cliff. A group of citizens standing nearby asks, "Why don't you push him off?" "The Nation's Eyes are on Chicago" was the title of another cartoon, which depicted a businessman rolling up his shirtsleeves while holding a sign saying "Chicago's Intolerable Crime Conditions." At the top of this cartoon, observers are watching with binoculars to see what the businessman is going to do to gangsters depicted at the bottom of the cartoon.[8]

By focusing public attention on twenty-eight notorious gangsters, Chamberlin forced a showdown. Who had the greater influence in Chicago—Al Capone or the Crime Commission? Behind which side was there stronger political pressure? Was Capone to be protected from the Crime Commission, representing the community, or was the community to be protected from Capone? Law-enforcing branches of government in Chicago were represented by the municipal police department, the Cook County sheriff's office, the state's attorney, and the U.S. district attorney. Was Capone too powerful for all of them?

Were his subordinate chieftains and lesser gang leaders beyond the reach of city, county, state, and federal authorities? Did the twenty-eight men, acknowledged by the Commission to be menaces to peace and order in the city, conduct their criminal enterprises with such skill that policemen, detectives, dry-law agents, and secret service men would forever remain baffled as to how to control them? Or was there protection that inhibited the law and paralyzed its strong arm? The sentiment of "decent and respectable" Chicago, as represented by the Crime Commission, insisted on action.

Civic organizations and religious groups threw their support behind the Commission.[9] Bank presidents announced they would refuse to accept deposits from public enemies; insurance company executives said they would quit issuing policies to gang leaders.[10] Twenty-eight gangsters had been put on the "spot." Still, the question remained: "Would the lawmakers and law enforcers act?"

State's Attorney Swanson pledged full aid, declaring: "This office will do everything in its power to run the hoodlums out of town. Of course, policing Chicago is a different question. We cannot do that. If the police department will make arrests, we will do the prosecuting."[11]

Federal Action

Action came fast from the federal government. Two days after U.S. Attorney George E. Q. Johnson received a letter from Chamberlin asking the government to assist in the public enemies drive, a jury found Ralph J. Capone guilty of tax fraud. Ralph, a younger brother of Al, and one of the "enemies" targeted by the Crime Commission, was convicted on four counts of attempting to defraud the United States out of income taxes.

Ralph Capone was the first of the public enemies to come to trial. A jury convicted him on one indictment of two counts charging attempts to defraud the government with false statements and concealment of assets. The maximum penalty on each of those felonies was ten years in prison and a $10,000 fine. The other indictment charged willful failure to pay income taxes and concealing facts in an offer in compromise that Ralph Capone had made to the government. The maximum penalty for each of those misdemeanors was one year in jail and a $10,000 fine.

This first indictment was not under an income tax statute, and in that respect Ralph Capone's case was unprecedented. Never before had anyone been tried under the general fraud statute for income tax delinquencies. Government testimony showed that Ralph Capone had deposited $1,871,000 in seven accounts under his own name and various aliases, at the Pinkert State Bank in Cicero, from 1924 to 1929. Officials from the Bureau of Internal Revenue estimated that Ralph Capone owed the government, in tax penalties and interest, more than $300,000. In his $1,000 offer in compromise, Capone had represented himself as an insolvent racehorse owner with assets consisting of a half interest in two horses. The government showed he had $25,000 on deposit at the time.

As part of Ralph Capone's defense, his lawyers described him as a gambler who sustained heavy losses in operating a race book. To refute this contention, the government put saloon keepers on the stand who told of buying quantities of beer at $55 a barrel from a Capone collector. In addition, clearinghouse sheets traced deposits to the bank accounts.

"The verdict is a great victory for the government," said U.S. Attorney Johnson. "Commendation is due the intelligence unit of the revenue department; A. P. Madden, the agent in charge; and his assistants who amassed overwhelming evidence under difficult conditions." Of the three assistant U.S. attorneys who prosecuted the case, Cassius Poust, Dwight H. Green, and Jacob Grossman, Johnson said, "No government officials ever rendered more faithful service.[12]

Local Inaction

In contrast to the federal government's decisive action against the public enemies, local authorities did nothing. Thrusting a hit list of gangsters beneath the noses of local officials failed to propel them into action. Two incidents show how lazy, corrupt, local criminal justice authorities lagged behind the federal government.

The first incident involved Myles O'Donnell, a public enemy, who was speeding in his sedan down the wrong side of Cicero Avenue and crashed into another car, killing one woman and injuring five other persons. After the state's attorney charged O'Donnell with manslaughter, the case slept on the criminal court calendars before being "dismissed for want of prosecution" on May 10. An assistant state's attorney told reporters that the case had to be dropped because police could not locate a key witness.

Following this announcement, Henry Barrett Chamberlin dispatched a private investigator to search for the missing witness. Twenty minutes later this investigator reported finding two witnesses instead of one.

"It's simple," the investigator said, "the records show that Hubert and Oscar F. Hanson, an extra witness, lived together at 2906 North Luna Avenue. Upon checking that address, I found Hubert had moved. Oscar was working at a printing establishment at 112 West Grand Avenue, the business address that we had for Hubert. Oscar told me Hubert was working for the Thompson-Zimmerman Printing Co. at 2225 West 11th Street, and I found him there."

To this Chamberlin added: "If the Crime Commission can find witnesses within twenty minutes to manslaughter allegedly committed by one of the twenty-eight public enemies, why can't the police do it?"[13]

The second incident consisted of a clash between Frank J. Loesch, the president of the Commission, and Cook County Sheriff John E. Traeger. Frustrated by Traeger's failure to respond to repeated Commission pleas to raid Capone's gambling joints in Cicero, Loesch went to the press. On May 21, Loesch told reporters that since December 31, 1928, the Commission had written fifty letters to Traeger concerning conditions in Cicero—giving detailed information as to locations of gambling places. "Although many of the smaller places have been closed," Loesch said, "the largest places remain open and attendance is so great that men stand six deep around the tables. Since illegal gambling is a fruitful source of income for the public enemies, your attention is again directed to closing these places."[14]

This public statement drew a response from Sheriff Traeger, who blamed the open and rampant gambling in Cicero on a shortage of policemen.[15] In view of the well-known political clout of Al Capone in Cicero, the ineffectiveness of Sheriff Traeger was more likely due to corrupt relations between Cook County officials and the underworld.

A Winner of an Idea

From April to September 1930, partly because of the Lingle shooting on June 9, but mainly because Capone had "paid off" so many local authorities, neither the police nor the prosecutors made any serious attempts to attack gangsters. To get the public enemies drive un-tracked, Chamberlin's friend and former secretary at the Municipal Voters' League, Judge John H. Lyle, hit upon a winner of an idea: Why not charge the leading gangsters with violating an 1871 vagrancy statute and hold them in jail on high bail bonds?

According to section 578 of chapter 38 of the Illinois criminal code,

persons who are habitually neglectful of their employment or their calling and do not lawfully provide for themselves or for the sup-port of their families, and all persons who are idle or dissolute and who neglect all lawful business and who habitually misspend their time by frequenting houses of ill fame, gaming houses, or tippling shops, are vagabonds whom it is the duty of the sheriff, bailiff of the municipal court of Chicago, constable, city marshal, and police to arrest upon warrant and bring before the nearest justice. On be-ing found guilty, the vagabond may be sentenced to hard labor for a term of not less than ten days nor more than six months.[16]

Upon reviewing the wording of this statute, Lyle concluded that the legislative intent was not limited to any special type of vagrant, the common or garden variety of hobo or village ne'er-do-well, who was a harmless individual. Even though the legislators of 1871 did not foresee the rise of the Prohibition gangster, their intent was to cover *all* individuals who were not supporting themselves by lawful means.

Lyle admitted there were differences between the persons charged with vagrancy in the late nineteenth century and the hoodlums of his day. The modern gangster had money, whereas the old vagrant had none; the old-time vagrant was not part of an organized group, while the modern gangster had borrowed the idea of organization from the business world. Moreover, the nineteenth-century vagrant did not wield any of the instruments of modern invention such as the machine gun, the bomb, and the automobile that the Prohibition gangster used. Yet, like the old-fashioned vagabond, the modern gangster was a parasite, contributing nothing to orderly society. And, although the modern gangster was far more vicious than the old-fashioned vagrant,

Lyle did not see that as a reason the discipline established for the lesser offender should not reach the gangster.

But how would this strategy affect Al Capone? Lyle foresaw these possibilities:

1. If Capone were arrested on a vagrancy warrant and declined to answer questions, a judge could find him guilty of vagrancy and fine him.

2. If Capone paid the fine, a judge could ask him to explain where the money had come from.

3. If Capone did not pay the fine, a judge could sentence him to the House of Correction to work out the fine.

4. If Capone revealed the actual sources of income, a grand jury could indict him for bootlegging and other crimes.

5. If Capone claimed legitimate employment, a grand jury could indict him for perjury.

6. If Capone testified in order to defend himself against a charge of vagrancy, U.S. Treasury agents could use this testimony to prosecute Capone for income tax evasion.[17]

Lyle met with his old friend and former boss at the Municipal Voters League, Henry Barrett Chamberlin. Lyle had served Chamberlin as secretary when Lyle was a twenty-year-old law student. Behind big horn-rimmed spectacles, Chamberlin's keen eyes sparkled as Lyle outlined the vagrancy attack. Chamberlin arranged an immediate conference with Frank J. Loesch, who happened to be Lyle's former law school instructor. Loesch enthusiastically approved Lyle's plan.

Chamberlin suggested that in issuing the vagrancy warrants Lyle should use the Commission's list of twenty-eight public enemies as a guide.[18] "Let us do everything possible to obtain wide public support for this action," said Chamberlin. "To coincide with the warrants, we'll reissue the list and send it to the newspapers and law enforcement officials. We'll urge every one to get behind the drive."[19]

Lyle's Vagrancy Drive

With Henry Barrett Chamberlin sitting on the bench next to him, Judge Lyle signed twenty-six vagrancy warrants on September 16. The list comprised the "public enemies" named in April by the Crime Commission minus two gangsters who authorities believed had been killed. Alphonse Capone, alias "Scarface" as he was called from the bench by Judge Lyle, and George ("Bugs") Moran, the rival of Capone, headed those named in the warrants.

Addressing newspaper reporters who had gathered in his court on account of a tip from Chamberlin that "an important announcement would be made," Lyle said:

> On April 24th, the Chicago Crime Commission—the only organiza-
> tion of its kind in the world—released a list of public enemies.
> These are men who have lived lives of crime and who have
> brought disgrace on this city both at home and abroad. Vagrancy
> warrants are the only method we have to reach these men. If we
> can keep them busy in court, they will not have time for crime.[20]

Lyle spoke for several minutes on the good deeds of the Crime Commission and endorsed the work being done by State's Attorney Swanson, Special Assistant State's Attorney Rathbun, and Chief Investigator Roche. The judge then called policeman Roy Van Herrick before him and praised him for arresting public enemies Moran and Mongoven. "I give you the honor of signing these complaints for the warrants," the judge said as he handed Van Herrick the complaints. "However, I take full responsibility for issuing the warrants."

As the late-afternoon session of court was about to end, Colonel Chamberlin spoke from the bench. He turned to Judge Lyle and told him the Crime Commission was in accord with what the judge was doing. Chamberlin assured Lyle that Frank J. Loesch, the president of the Crime Commission, stood behind the vagrancy drive.[21]

When police officials at the detective bureau received the twenty-six warrants, radio dispatchers broadcast to all squad cars the names and descriptions of the twenty-six men wanted. Dispatchers also informed cops on automobile patrol that Police Commissioner Alcock would give "creditable mention and special consideration" for bringing any of the gangsters in. Spurred on by this radio message, thirty-eight squad cars—seven of them from the detective bureau—and one hundred station flivvers toured the city's streets continuously on September 17.

Despite this flurry of police activity, the only public enemy on whom the police served a vagrancy warrant was Danny Stanton, who happened to be in a cell at the detective bureau when Judge Lyle issued the warrants. But Stanton was walking the streets again that night, having been charged with gun toting and released on a bond of $515,400.

To explain why they hadn't brought in the most famous of the twenty-six gangsters named in Judge Lyle's warrants, police officials declared that Al Capone had only been in town once since Jake Lingle's murder and that he had remained only five days. They believed he was in Florida and that he had in his retinue no fewer than six of those wanted on vagrancy warrants—Ralph Capone, Tony Volpe, Frank Rio, "Machine Gun" Jack McGurn, Frank Diamond, and Jake Guzik. Further, police pointed out that "Bugs" Moran and Joseph Aiello had been hiding ever since the Lingle killing and that Leo Mongoven had also been missing. Mongoven was either with Moran or with the Capone outfit in Florida. According to law enforcement officials, Frankie Lake and Terry Druggan were in the ice business in Detroit, while "Polack Joe" Saltis was living on his $100,000 estate, with its private eighteen-hole golf course in northwestern Wisconsin. Chief of Detectives Norton was positive that some gangsters were going about their business as usual, among them "Three Fingered Jack" White and George Barker, the labor union racketeers; the brothers Frank and Vincent McErlane; William ("Klondike") and Myles O'Donnell and James ("Fur") Sammons, who used to peddle beer on the west side but now were involved in labor union rackets; and Edward ("Spike") O'Donnell of the south side O'Donnells, who was frequenting the Back of the Yards district.[22]

Judge Lyle arraigned Danny Stanton on a vagrancy charge on September 18. Stanton's attorney, Thomas Nash, immediately asked for a change of venue, which Lyle eventually granted. But before that, the lawyer objected to the judge's allowing the prosecutor to present what Nash termed "irrelevant evidence."

"Don't interrupt me," said Judge Lyle to Mr. Nash. "I'm not going to be pushed around by lawyers who, no matter how high their reputation, have been representing the underworld in court."[23]

Shortly after Judge Lyle had arraigned Stanton, he called Chamberlin, Rathbun, Roche, and several newspaper reporters into his chambers. Judge Lyle revealed to them that four attorneys representing "Scarface Al" Capone had been in to see him, seeking to arrange for Capone's surrender on the vagrancy warrant. The lawyers wanted an agreement that their client would not be mussed up by being thrown into a cell and that he would be permitted to go free on bail. Judge Lyle said he told the lawyers he would make no promises. Finally, the judge announced to the press that in the trials of the twenty-six gangsters for vagrancy, the people of Chicago would be represented in court officially by Rathbun, Roche, and Swanson, and unofficially by Chamberlin.[24]

"The gangsters," Lyle said, "will be represented by their paid criminal lawyers, who feed, fatten, and thrive on large fees from these despicable characters. Legal technicalities, criminal politics, and dishonest public officials have made the streets of Chicago safe for murdering gangsters but now the battle is moved from the streets to the courts where the weapons will be law books instead of machine guns."[25]

Police Scandal

A sensational scandal broke out involving the police department and public enemies on September 26. Federal officers, searching for Frank Nitti, Capone bookkeeper and treasurer, who was under federal indictment for income tax evasion, raided a south side hotel known as a hangout for members of the Capone gang. Arthur P. Madden and Clarence Converse of the special intelligence unit of the Bureau of Internal Revenue led the raid, which took them through the five-story Carlson Hotel at 2138 South Wabash Avenue.

From top to bottom the agents and two detective bureau squads roamed the place, encountering thirteen men and a bevy of women but no gangsters. Working down from the top floor, Converse finally arrived at room 204. Within that room was Tony Tagenti, a Capone bondsman, who said he was lying down because he was suffering from influenza. Searching for a gun, Converse slid his hand beneath Tagenti's pillow and withdrew a folded police memorandum. Converse scanned the police list and asked, "Where did you get this?"[26]

"I don't know a thing about it," said Tagenti. "This is my office here, but I didn't even know that thing was around."

Appearing on the list were the names of forty-one hoodlums whom Police Commissioner Alcock had personally targeted for arrest. Beside the name of each gangster were the names of the policemen who had arrested that gangster before and who would be expected to do so again, the next time serving a new vagabond warrant. Crosses had been written in pencil opposite the names of eight of the men on the list.

Converse took the document to the detective bureau where Deputy Chief Ryan said it was a copy of a memo he had dictated on September 18 and of which he had ordered four copies made. Two of the copies, Ryan said, were for his own office, one for Chief Norton, and another for a newly formed vagrancy bureau in the state's attorney's office. Ryan said his two copies were safe. He declared he had taken one to Chief Norton, who directed him to give it and the remaining copy to attorney William Luthhardt, head of the vagrancy bureau.

Acting Police Commissioner Alcock then accused an unnamed spy of delivering into the hands of Capone gangsters the secret list of notorious hoodlums slated for prosecution for vagrancy. Rumors circulated about the police department that not only was there a spy in the department but that the list had been taken to members of the Capone gang, perhaps to "Scarface Al" himself, and that Capone had censored the list by marking crosses next to certain names. After the eight names had been marked for deletion from the list, Capone exerted influence to cause a new list to be prepared omitting the eight names plus two others. Each of the eight belonged to the Capone gang: some had records as Capone killers and all were admitted by the police to be among the worst criminals on the entire list. No names left on the list were recognizable as those of prominent Capone gangsters.

Chief of Detectives Norton and his deputy chief, John Ryan, asserted that the original was stolen from patrolman William Balswick's desk and that when the patrolman made up a new list, he did so from memory. Balswick said that he had forgotten to include the names of the eight Capone gangsters. As for the theft of the original list, the patrolman claimed that "some newspaperman probably took it."[27]

The original list of hoodlums targeted for vagrancy prosecutions was prepared September 17, after Chief Norton had informed Deputy Chief Ryan that Acting Commissioner Alcock desired to wage a war of his own on gangsters and had ordered the preparation of a list of likely hoodlums to be arrested by the police. Thumbing through the pictures of the notorious gangsters, bound in a special volume at the detective bureau, Ryan and Balswick prepared a list of forty-one names. They submitted the list to Norton who suggested that the names of the officers who had previously arrested the hoodlums be included in the list. Balswick then inserted the policemen's names, made a new draft and three carbon copies, and locked them up in his desk. The next morning Balswick discovered that the original and three copies were missing, and after searching for them, he made up a new list from memory. Four copies of this were struck off, Balswick said, one being retained in his own files, another going to Norton, and two being delivered to the assistant city attorney, William Luth-ardt, the prosecutor in charge of the vagrancy drive. All those copies were accounted for, according to police officials.[28]

The list found in Tagenti's bed was the original of the set typed by Balswick. In pencil markings on the margin, crosses had been made before the names of the eight Capone gangsters whose names did not appear on the new list. Norton construed the omission of these names to mean that the spy who had stolen the first list had obtained access to the second list and had notified the Capone gangsters of those who had been omitted. But two others, who did not belong to the Capone gang, were also omitted from the second list, and their names were not marked with the crosses. Those two men were Maurice and Frank Quirk, both beer runners. The Capone gangsters whose names were not on the list that was finally approved and sent to judges in order to secure vagrancy warrants were:

Louis Campagna, known as a Capone killer: he was arrested in 1928 in front of the old South Clark Street police station with two .45-caliber automatics strapped to his waist at a time when the authorities were about to release Capone enemy, Joe Aiello, from custody at that station.

Claude Maddox, owner of the Circus Cafe, where the St. Valentine's Day Massacre was plotted.

Ted Newberry, Zuta-Moran-Aiello lieutenant, who switched to the Capone gang and took charge of Capone's north side booze traffic.

Tony Accardo, a Capone murderer, who was arrested in a Checker cab with "Machine Gun" Jack McGurn.

Sam Hunt, who was arrested after a machine-gun assault upon an Aiello henchman.

Marty Guilfoyle, operator of gambling enterprises on the northwest side for the Capone gang.

Murray Humphries, a labor racketeer enlisted by the Caponeites to help in the seizure of labor unions.

Tony Cappizzio, a Capone racketeer associated with Maddox in the operation of the Circus Cafe.[29]

Two grand juries and a committee of aldermen investigated the circumstances surrounding the police lists, but this mystery was never solved. The grand juries brought out that the police had neglected to question Tagenti, the Capone bondsman in whose custody the list was found, and that Chief of Detectives Norton had hurried Tagenti through the bureau of identification at the detective bureau.[30] The only questioning of Tagenti on the subject of the secret police list was done by Clarence Converse, ace of the federal special intelligence outfit, to whom Tagenti professed complete ignorance of how the list came to be nestling under his pillow.[31]

"My Secret Ambition"

Judge Lyle's vagrancy campaign expressed for many Chicagoans in a dramatic manner their own deep feelings about the public enemies. In the heart of the average citizen, not at all anxious to face the gangsters of the underworld in person, Lyle's daily skirmishes with gangsters were looked upon as "My Secret Ambition."

Take the day when public enemy James ("Fur") Sammons stood with bowed head in the crowded little courtroom at the Chicago Avenue police station. He had stood boldly at first but wilted when Judge Lyle put him under a bond of $50,000 for a vagrancy charge. Sammons was a rapist, murderer, and gunman, who had been notorious in his defiance of the law. Another arrest meant little to him.[32]

"Why are you gunmen afraid to look me in the eye?" asked Judge Lyle. "Look up!"

Sammons still hung his head.

"Look up or I'll send you to jail for six months for contempt," Lyle commanded.

The eyes that had looked upon many a victim without mercy at last were raised to the face of Judge Lyle.

"It's time for men of your stripe to get out of Chicago," said Lyle.[33]

Not a judicial sentence, but a thought that echoed in thousands of hearts.

"I've heard that before," sneered Sammons.

Judge Lyle said slowly and deliberately, as if he were delivering a prison sentence: "It will be a long time before you quit this territory. You are going to be put behind bars until you forget how to use a gun."[34]

Next, attorney Everett Jennings, representing Sammons, attempted to speak.

"I don't want to hear a word out of you," said Judge Lyle.

"I just wanted to speak a word for the Constitution of the United States," said the lawyer.

"The Constitution doesn't need criminal lawyer defenders," retorted Lyle. "The only time you consider the Constitution is when you're trying to get around, under, or through it."

A prejudiced judge certainly. There had not even been a trial. Lyle's prediction about Sammons being put behind bars, however, proved true. A few weeks later Sammons was not only found guilty of vagrancy in another court but was sent back to the penitentiary to serve out a sentence of murder—a sentence that was found in still another court to have been shortened illegally by parole. How different had been Sammons's experience in other police courts, where continuances and disappearing witnesses had worn out more serious charges against him. Yet, this episode typified Lyle's unique style: high bonds, colorful language addressed personally to individual gangsters, and persistent efforts to send them to the rock pile.

"Vigorous and independent, but lacking in judicial temperament," the Chicago Bar Association said of him.[35]

To which the judge replied: "If judicial temperament means that I should be lenient with gangsters instead of severe, then I am glad that I am lacking in it. I refuse to mollycoddle criminals with lengthy records."[36]

Lyle cut loose with a stream of intemperate remarks during Ralph Capone's vagrancy hearing in the judge's court on October 9. Capone was free on bond, waiting for an appellate court to decide whether or not he would go to prison. "What! Courtesy to a Capone!" he exclaimed, when attorneys for Ralph Capone sought to have him put in the custody of a bailiff instead of being handled in the ordinary manner. "Courtesy to a Capone! To a man who with his brother heads a gang of criminals the likes of which the world has never known. He'll be handled like any common criminal." And so Lyle sent the second in command in the Capone organization to be fingerprinted, photographed, questioned, and "pushed around" as he had never been before.

"Cut out the bunk," Ralph Capone told the police, but later he asked for a change of venue from Judge Lyle's court on the grounds that the judge was prejudiced against him. Admitting his bias, Lyle granted the motion. Capone was released on a $10,000 bond but found other troubles awaiting him when an appellate court upheld his conviction for income tax evasion.[37]

Judge Lyle also raked over the two Guziks. The Guziks were Capone men who had enjoyed immunity from the law. Harry Guzik had been convicted as a panderer, but Governor Len Small had pardoned him. The Guziks appeared in Judge Lyle's court on charges that seemed of little consequence to them.

"Your very appearance in the courts which you have hitherto scorned is significant," said Lyle to the swarthy brothers as they stood before him. "It indicates a surrender to the three million people who have lived in mortal terror of you and your associates."

"You, Harry Guzik," said Lyle, "are a big, fat, healthy man, and you've never done a day of work. I hear that you lived off prostitution all your life. I don't get a kick out of punishing people, but I do relish the opportunity of being a judge when such men as you two, living off vice and crime, fattening on blood money, are brought before me. The worst of it is that you men are smart. Capone has to have such men around him in order to succeed."

After this outburst, Lyle granted the Guziks' request for a change of venue. "You Capone men are through," Lyle said. "The public has been callous to the activities of gangsters. It has almost given up hope. But now, with the aid of the press, this movement has started."

Judge Lyle aimed more tough talk at "Scarface Al" himself. "We will send Capone to the electric chair if it is possible to do so," he told Chicago newspaper reporters. "He deserves to die. Capone has become almost a mythical being in Chicago. He is not a myth but a reptile. He is more than a concentrated crime wave. He is a real and powerful political force. Capone has no right to live."[38]

But Lyle couldn't talk Capone into court, and the police couldn't locate him to serve the vagrancy warrant. Where the police failed, Henry Barrett Chamberlin and the Crime Commission succeeded.

Chamberlin assigned an investigator to track down Capone. Within a few days, the investigator found Capone watching a football game between Morton High School of Cicero and Harrison High of Chicago at 59th Court and 24th Street. Capone, at play, was surrounded by six bodyguards. Murmurs of "There's Al Capone" and "Look at his bodyguards" ran through the crowd. The Crime Commission investigator saw two uniformed Cicero policemen standing about, but they seemed oblivious to Capone's presence.[39]

Although Chamberlin at least had solved the mystery of Capone's whereabouts, this was of small benefit to Chicago police who sought to serve him with the vagrancy warrant issued by Judge Lyle. As Chamberlin pointed out, the Chicago police could not go beyond the city limits with a municipal court warrant, and the Cicero police could not arrest the gangster and turn him over to Chicago authorities.

Thwarting Popular Justice

Just as Chamberlin's public enemies drive started to show some muscle, a few judges, feeling bound by the rule of law, put themselves in the way of popular justice. While considering the pleas of two gunmen, Judges Harry M. Fisher and Joseph B. David stated that they would not be part of the "howling mob trampling on legal precedents and traditions."[40] Ruling on the "means" used against the enemies, judges sitting on the Illinois Supreme Court put the skids on the vagrancy drive.

Acting on a writ of habeas corpus for James ("Fur") Sammons whose bond Judge Lyle had set at $50,000, the Illinois Supreme Court on October 16 reduced the bond to $5,000.[41] The court held that "bail must be reasonable and sufficient only to insure the attendance of the defendant at trial." Furthermore, the court inferred that bail could not be set so high as to deny its benefits to anyone, be that person an ordinary citizen or a "public enemy."[42]

Similarly, in another vagrancy case involving a public enemy, the Illinois Supreme Court stressed that due process of law should not be compromised even under circumstances where the government claimed that law and order had broken down. In this case, James Belcastro, a public enemy, had been convicted as a vagabond in Chicago Municipal Court and sentenced to six months in jail. Official charges against Belcastro asserted that he was a habitual law violator and that he was reputed to be an associate of James Catura, who was also reputed to be a habitual law violator. In setting Belcastro free, the Illinois Supreme Court ruled part of the Illinois vagrancy law was unconstitutional because "it sought to punish an individual for what he was reputed to be, regardless of what he actually did."[43]

Following these rulings, Henry Barrett Chamberlin issued this public statement in support of Judge Lyle's methods:

> The Chicago Crime Commission realizes there are times when criminal justice must be based upon expediency, necessity, and public peace; that in an abnormal crime situation normal institutions are not always workable. There is no other way to deal with a certain class of criminals than to break them to pieces or they will break you.[44]

The business community stood by Lyle. Whenever Judge Lyle attended meetings of various businessmen's clubs, his listeners assured him of their support in his upcoming bid for reelection to the municipal court. In a statement addressed to "the people of Chicago," signed by Loesch, and dated October 23, 1930, the Commission noted the progress being made in the war against public enemies. "Into this critical situation," the statement read, "has come a judge of vigor and independence who has given voice to and made manifest the aspirations of the law abiding. He has interpreted legal technicalities in the interests of criminal justice. He deserves the support of the decent citizens."[45]

When voters went to the polls on November 4, they demonstrated their support for Lyle by reelecting the crusading judge.

Capone-Hunting

Chamberlin and Lyle kept their sights fixed on Capone. But the gang leader surfaced only in the news. On October 24, police mentioned Capone's name in connection with the murder of Joe Aiello, north side alcohol king, partner of George ("Bugs") Moran, and public enemy. Aiello had stepped into a carefully laid trap and was caught in a murderous cross fire that streamed from two gun nests at Komar and West End avenues, a mile west of Garfield Park. Thirty steel-coated bullets ended the career of Aiello, who was one of Al Capone's bitterest foes.

Police and prosecutors blamed the slaying on Capone. They pointed to the known hostility between the two men and the perfect arrangements made by the assassins to get Aiello. They asserted the machine guns were Capone weapons and the camouflaged nests were trademarks of Capone precision. The Aiello killing, detectives were certain, was a Capone job.[46]

On November 4, Chief Justice John P. McGoorty of the criminal court revealed that a representative of Al Capone had approached him with a proposal to compromise with "Al Brown." The offer came through Michael J. Galvin, secretary and treasurer of the Chicago teamsters and chauffeurs' union. Galvin suggested that "Brown" would be willing to call off his racketeers if the judge would guarantee that he could peddle beer unmolested by the authorities. McGoorty told him, "No deal."[47]

On November 14, Congressman Stanley Kunz, a Democrat from the Eighth Illinois District, charged through the newspapers that Capone had engineered his defeat by Peter C. Granata, a Republican. With the Republican control of Congress hanging in the balance and with every vote in the Republican ranks of paramount importance, each congressman stood in a position of unusual power. In discussing the Kunz charges, politicians jested about the possibility of Capone holding the balance of power in Congress.

Congressman Kunz reported that he was gathering evidence in affidavit form through the six wards in his district, which was located on the west side of Chicago and included part of the bloody Twentieth Ward bossed by Morris Eller. Kunz asserted that solely on the basis of straight Democratic tickets voted he should have won by about 10,000 votes. "My friends tell me," said Kunz, "that Capone gangsters, four or five to every precinct, used threats and gunplay where money could not buy them votes. I have election officials who will make affidavits that they were coerced by hoodlums with guns into marking Granata votes on straight Democratic tickets. There is one Italian precinct where friends of mine are ready to prove that 220 straight Democratic tickets were votes—yet by my count there was twelve."[48]

Capone's name popped up again in a story about threats made

against the makers of grape concentrates. Donald Conn, managing director of the company, received information that Capone was displeased about his intent to sell bottled grape concentrate in Illinois and that Conn's health would suffer if he persisted with the plan.[49] Rumors of the presence of "Scarface Al" near Conn's home in southern California sent heads of law enforcement agencies into a secret conference where they planned action against what they termed "an invasion by Chicago gangsters." A Los Angeles district attorney promised "to get Capone out of California," but detectives in that state searched in vain for the gang leader.[50]

Capone bathed in the limelight of the press. "CAPONE FEEDS HUNGRY: EVEN A GANG CHIEF HAS A HEART" proclaimed a headline in late November. The story described a big building in the Loop bearing the sign "Free Food for the Workless." Two thousand were fed there on a single day on stew, soup, bread, and coffee. No churches were involved. Inquirers were told that a well-known philanthropist who wished to do good by stealth was behind the project. The manager of this soup kitchen admitted that Al Capone was paying all the expenses and that his lieutenants were giving their services as relief workers. Capone, it was reported, believed that persons of wealth like himself should take the responsibility of feeding the poor in these hard times.[51]

Fed up with reading about Capone in the newspapers, Lyle personally went looking for the man who had ingratiated himself with the public through stories such as the one about the soup kitchen. Accompanied by Chief Investigator Pat Roche, Assistant State's Attorney Charles F. Rathbun, and Special U.S. Intelligence Officer Clarence Converse, Lyle led a raid on three Capone hideaways in Berwyn but missed the gang chief.[52]

Capone's trail led to New York. Railroad detectives informed officials of Duchess County, New York, that Al Capone and three Italians had detrained from a New York Central flyer at Poughkeepsie, New York, on December 8. Capone and his companions were met at the station by a large sedan, which whisked them away toward Manhattan. The *Tribune* quoted Chicago law enforcement authorities as believing Capone would hide in Brooklyn, where his friend Johnny Torrio had been living for four years. Chicago authorities speculated that Capone had gone into hiding because of the campaign against public enemies and the federal government's efforts to convict him of income tax evasion.[53]

U.S. District Attorney George E. Q. Johnson joined the hunt on December 13, issuing a summons to Capone to appear in court in Chicago before December 15. If Capone appeared in response to the summons, officials from the Cook County state's attorney's office planned to serve him with one of Lyle's vagrancy warrants. The action upon which Capone was summoned to federal court involved him in a contempt of court action that was two years old. Capone had been cited for contempt of court for failure to submit to questioning before a federal grand jury in connection with the investigation of a Chicago Heights liquor ring. He had been at liberty under a bond of $5,000. Should Capone fail to appear on the fifteenth, U.S. District Attorney Johnson said he would ask for the forfeiture of Capone's bond and for the issuance of an arrest warrant. Johnson predicted that federal agents would be able to find Capone and serve the warrant.[54]

But Capone never appeared on December 15. Capone's attorneys argued that he didn't have to appear because the charge against him was a misdemeanor and not a felony. Both prosecutors and defense lawyers agreed upon January 19 as the new trial date.[55]

Lyle was determined to get Capone. "We will send Capone to the electric chair for murdering Colosimo," the judge said. "He deserves to die; he has no right to live." After ventilating his feelings toward Capone, Lyle turned his attention to the future: "The World's Fair of 1933 will be a failure unless Capone is exterminated."[56]

Lyle's Bid for Mayor

With Capone still free and roaming about, Judge Lyle unwrapped a present for "Scarface Al" and his political protector, Mayor Thompson. Describing himself as a foe of "Caponeism in government," Lyle announced his candidacy for the Republican nomination for mayor of Chicago. This pitted him against Thompson and Alderman Arthur Albert.

Chamberlin and the Crime Commission backed Lyle. In Chamberlin's view, capturing the mayor's office would afford the Crime Commission more leeway in pursuing the public enemies than if Lyle continued to sit on the bench. Chamberlin thought that if Lyle were elected mayor the police might be inclined to take orders from Judge Lyle instead of Al Capone.[57]

Local prosecutors supported Lyle's candidacy. Assistant States Attorney Harry Ditchburne released to the press an inventory of Lyle's accomplishments. The most noteworthy among them was the incarceration of three of the most notorious hoodlums and racketeers in Chicago. Two of them, George ("Red") Barker and James ("Fur") Sammons, were now in prison on felony charges, and a third, William J. ("Three Fingered Jack") White, was facing possible electrocution for murder.

"Judge Lyle's vagrancy drive has accomplished two things which are of inestimable value to the prosecuting authorities and the police," read Ditchburne's press release. "The first is that he stripped the leading criminals of the community of their false glamour and showed them up for what they are—ordinary thieves, robbers, and graduated keepers of houses of prostitution. The second is that he has created a public sentiment which has taken away from the criminals the deference shown to them in the past when they were arrested and taken into the courts."

Part of the release described the conduct of the big shots of gangland when taken into Judge Lyle's court. It noted how they cringed and begged for mercy. It stated that whenever they were taken before Lyle they started to "whimper" for jury trials or changes of venue, anything to get out of Lyle's court. According to the press release, Lyle's campaign had "struck panic into the ranks of Chicago's gangs and demonstrated to them that they were social outcasts." Before Lyle's drive, it had been customary for many public officials to curry favor with the hoodlum chiefs—some even to truckle to them—with the consequence that many favors were given them that the smaller fry in crime did not enjoy. On account of the vagrancy drive, criminals, who once swaggered into the courts and were the recipients of deference by court functionaries and even some judges, were made to feel that they were powerless, despicable characters. All departments and agencies of Chicago government were now awake to the serious problem of organized crime, and the public was aroused as never before.

Two other effects of the vagrancy drive were outlined in the press release. As a result of the high bonds set by Judge Lyle for vagrants, other judges were now following the same policy. The state supreme court practically upheld the high bond policy, according to the release, when it set $5,000 as the bail for Sammons on a vagrancy charge. Before that, the usual bond was $400. Another result was that paying large bail bonds handicapped the criminals financially so that instead of being defended by the best attorneys, they had to go to court with less capable lawyers.[58]

If Lyle's political campaign had been half as effective as the vagrancy drive, he might have won. Going on the offensive, Lyle charged that the Capone gang gave $50,000 to the Thompson campaign fund in 1927 and that in return Thompson appointed Daniel A. Serritella, one of Capone's closest associates, city sealer.

"The real issue in this race," said Judge Lyle, "is not whether I shall be elected or whether Thompson shall be elected, but whether Al Capone is to be authorized to rule Chicago again through the medium of a dummy in the mayor's chair."[59]

Frank J. Loesch of the Crime Commission issued a press release on February 16, claiming Lyle's estimate was too conservative. Capone actually contributed a total of $260,000 in the primary and election campaigns to insure the election of Thompson in 1927. The deal, according to Loesch, was that Capone should have the right to run houses of prostitution and gambling places and to sell beer and booze in all the territory of the city south of Madison street.[60]

While Lyle was attacking the Capone influence in city hall, a body-guard of two motorcycle policemen accompanied him night and day. Upon finishing his first day under police guard, Lyle turned to his two police escorts.

"Go back and tell Chief Alcock," Lyle said, "not to worry about me. Tell him to worry about Capone. There is a warrant I issued and it hasn't been served. Tell Alcock to get service on that warrant. I'll take care of myself."[61]

Lyle's political allies thought the apprehension of Capone would swing votes to the judge in the election on the following day so Judge Frank Padden ordered investigator Patrick Roche to find Capone and serve the vagrancy warrant. Roche's squads visited all the gangster's usual haunts but returned empty-handed late in the day on February 23.

Political news temporarily stole the limelight away from the search for Capone when Republican voters renominated Thompson on February 24. Votes for Alderman Albert split the opposition to Thompson, thus allowing "Big Bill" to win in spite of the fact that he failed to receive fifty percent of all Republican votes. In the Democratic primary, Anton Cermak piled up 235,260 votes to gain his party's nomination.[62]

Capone's Trial for Vagrancy

Capone finally surrendered on the vagrancy warrant. It happened on February 25 in the federal building in Chicago. As Capone left the U.S. district courtroom at the close of the morning session of his trial for contempt, police Sergeants Edward Tyrrell and Joseph Hacksaw served the vagrancy warrant and then hurried Capone to the detective bureau. After fingerprinting and photographing "Scarface Al," detectives questioned him, gave him coffee, and fed him sandwiches. Capone's lawyers scheduled property valued at $50,000 at 4639 North Albany Avenue, and Capone was free within a few minutes. Arraignment on the vagrancy charge was set for February 24, but Capone's lawyers asked for and received a continuance until March 4.

Back in federal court for the afternoon session, Capone was found guilty of contempt. Judge James Wilkerson sentenced him to six months in jail and then released the gangster on postconviction bail.[63]

Capone finally appeared in municipal court on March 4 for his long-awaited trial for vagrancy. Decked out in a blue chinchilla overcoat and flanked by fifteen police detectives, Capone entered the rear door of the criminal court building and strolled into Judge Frank Padden's courtroom. A crowd consisting largely of women tried to break into the anteroom of the court to steal a glimpse of Public Enemy Number One.

"Al Brown, Alphonse Capone, or Scarface Al," a clerk boomed, as he called the case.

Michael Ahern, Capone's lawyer, leaped to his feet. "I ask that the epithet 'Scarface Al,' which appears on this complaint be stricken from the record." Capone vigorously nodded his approval.

"My client's name is Alphonse Capone," said Ahern. "He wants it understood he is not Scarface Al, or anything else but Alphonse Capone."[64]

Judge Padden told the clerk to strike the alias and nickname from the warrant and ordered the case continued until March 20. As the official proceedings ended, newspaper photographers begged for a shot of Capone before the bench. A mad scramble ensued with other persons trying to get into the picture with Capone. Cameras equipped with audio machines were set up, but Judge Padden called a halt to the picture-taking session before the cameras started to roll. Capone exited through the rear door of the court and drove off in his own auto, followed by two squads of cars.

By March 20, charges against Capone had been amended and now he stood accused of "prowling about disorderly houses, gambling joints, railroad stations and brokerage houses without any visible means of support."[65] According to a Crime Commission observer who was present in Judge Padden's court on March 20, defense counsel Ahern objected to the filing of the complaint against Capone. Ahern stated that the complaint was sworn to by Roy Van Herrick and that, therefore, the court should examine Van Herrick to determine whether or not there was probable cause to hold Capone.

The judge ordered the policeman sworn in. Van Herrick, according to the Crime Commission observer, testified that he knew Capone and that everything sworn to in the complaint signed by him was "upon his information and belief and not based upon his personal knowledge."[66]

Upon hearing this, Judge Padden said, "It is obvious that the complaining witness does not know anything about this defendant. Capone is known throughout the United States, and surely there is some police officer who knows about Capone based on personal knowledge. I will give you, the prosecution, time to get such an officer." Judge Padden continued the Capone vagrancy case until April 3.

The old pull had not departed. Getting Capone behind bars was like trying to catch fish between wet fingers. On the third, Judge Padden ordered the assistant state's attorney to produce a Chicago policeman who could swear of his own knowledge that Capone was indeed a vagrant. Since no policeman would testify against Capone, the state dropped the charges against him.[67] As Capone left the courtroom on April 3, he told reporters complacently, "Biggest frame-up I ever knew."[68]

"Never Quit"

Capone's courtroom victory set back Henry Barrett Chamberlin's public enemies drive. Judge Justin F. McCarthy drove another nail into the coffin containing the corpse of the campaign when he forced the state's attorney on June 4 to drop vagrancy charges against two more public enemies. Those appearing in court were Rocco Fanelli, Capone henchman, and Edward ("Spike") O'Donnell, south side beer runner.[69] The state entered nolle prosses in both cases, declaring that it had no evidence on which to support vagrancy charges.[70]

The *Chicago Post* even published this "obituary" for the vagrancy drive:

> Many friends in Chicago were saddened to learn of the demise to-day of Judge Lyle's Vagrancy Drive, a sterling citizen who has been ailing recently. The drive suffered many severe hemorrhages during the last year and rapidly lost vitality. The end came in Justin F. McCarthy's court today when two operations were performed, removing the last vestiges of the infirm gentleman.[71]

I'll never quit pursuing Capone," said Henry Barrett Chamberlin when asked by reporters whether his public enemies drive was still alive. "Besides," he added, "the record proves how effective the enemies drive has been."

As of June 1931, the status of the public enemies was as follows:

Incarcerated in prison or jail	5
Convicted and under sentence	4
Convicted and awaiting sentence	1
Ordered extradited	1
Ordered deported	1
Killed	2
Awaiting judgment	1
Fugitives	5
Cleared of Charges	8

Ignoring the fact that more enemies fell into the "cleared of charges" category than any of the other categories, Chamberlin hailed the public enemies program as a success. He promised to continue the campaign "until every one of the original twenty-eight is punished or driven from this community."

True to his word, Chamberlin launched an attack on a second group of public enemies. He designated twenty-eight more men as public enemies and released their names to the press on August 1, 1931. Chamberlin sent copies of the new list to Chief Justice Sonsteby of the municipal court, State's Attorney Swanson, U.S. Attorney Johnson, Sheriff Meyering, and acting Police Commissioner Alcock. The men named in the new list were considered second-rate gangsters and hoodlums at the time the first list was published; however, some of the newcomers, such as Ted Newberry, had become gang chiefs since then.

Just as before, Chamberlin supplied Chicago newspapers with pictures of twenty-eight public enemies, and the newspapers published all of them.[72] And just as before, whenever one of those listed was arrested, he was identified in the newspapers as a "public enemy." This time, however, the *Herald and Examiner* gave a new twist to the public enemies story. After checking police files for the records of the men whose names were on the list, the *Herald and Examiner* reported that there were no records at the detective bureau for eighteen of the men in this new group.[73] A check of records at the police department's bureau of identification showed no information on men who had trials in as many as three murders, others who had been convicted of felonies and were facing sentences, and still others who faced trial on pending indictments.

Editors of the *Herald and Examiner* dramatized the significance of the information missing from the police files in an editorial that contrasted the crimes committed by the men on the Crime Commission's second list with a case police officials had pressed against a man in July 1931. In the latter case, the "infallible" police record system exposed an old man as having served a penitentiary sentence in 1892. The old man, who was a father, had pulled his Spanish War saber off the wall to resist detectives serving him with a warrant for menacing actions he had made the day before in a quarrel between neighbors. Detectives took the old man, along with his two sons, to the police bureau where it was discovered that he had served two years in prison for forgery in 1892. After disgracing the old man in the eyes of two grown sons who were ignorant of their father's past, the police released the "heart-broken" man so he could return to leading a life of exemplary conduct.[74]

The *Herald and Examiner* asked its readers why police files refused to admit the existence of eighteen of the men on the Crime Commissions's second list when the library of the *Herald and Examiner* showed a detailed record of the criminal careers of the same men. Then it listed the "high points" in the accomplishments of these gangsters.

Mike McGovern, McErlane beer runner; tried three times for murder; arrested twice for murderous assaults; arrested once for bombing; arrested once for robbery.

Anthony ("Red") Kissane, ex-bodyguard of the late "Jake" Lingle, *Tribune* reporter; convicted and facing sentence of a year and a fine of $1000 for gun-toting; tried for the murder of William Newman and the wounding of seven others in a brawl; arrested for two robberies; arraigned for murder; identified as a bomber; tried for vagrancy.

Harry ("Greasy Thumb") Guzik, Capone Loop collector; convicted as a panderer in 1922, pardoned by Governor Small; tried for vagrancy; indicted and facing trial for income tax evasion.

Marty Guilfoyle, northwest side slot machine king; charged with operating many illegal gambling places.

Henry Finkelstein, fined $500 for operating distilleries; suspect in slaying of Jack Zuta; arrested in brewery raid.

Charles Fischetti, cousin of Al Capone; identified as a slugger; charged with operating illegal gambling places.

Eddie Kaufman, "brains" of the McErlane beer mob; tried for fixing the jury in the trial of Governor Small at Waukegan; arrested in holdup; fined $1000 for beer running; suspect in murder of "Dingbat" Oberta in 1930.

Ted Newberry, Capone north side chief; under indictment at Peoria for liquor conspiracy; facing trial as public enemy under vagrancy law, indicted for murder; identified with Frank Foster as buying the revolver used to kill "Jake" Lingle; suspect in two shootings; arraigned for gun-toting.

Nick Kramer, guard for Joe Saltis; suspect in robbery case; arrested countless times.

Joe Fusco, Capone new Chief; indicted with sixty-seven other Capone gangsters for liquor Conspiracy.

Sam Campagnia, "Little New York," Capone gunman; identified as slayer of Frankie Yale in Brooklyn; indicted for robbery.

Grover Dullard, north side gambling organizer; tried for bribing jurors.

Jim Genna, former head of the six Genna brothers alky mob; suspect in murders of Dion O'Banion and Hymie Weiss; arraigned for murder; jailed for robbing a church.

Joe Cainski, Spike O'Donnell gangster; investigated by the grand jury for gun toting; arraigned for assault.

Paddy Sullivan, ex-policeman discharged for taking bribes; served thirty days in jail for beer-running; tried for murder.

James L. Quigley, Spike O'Donnell henchman; tried for murder; arrested for another murder.

Tony Accardo, pal of Jack McGurn and Capone killer; suspect in killings of Joe Aiello, Jack Zuta, and "Mike de Pike" Heitler; convicted of gun toting.

Bernard O'Donnell, brother of Klondike: tried twice for gun toting; tried for perjury.[75]

These were the unofficial records of eighteen of the twenty-eight men on the second list of public enemies. Yet there was no way of knowing from the detective bureau records that the eighteen were anything less than choirboys.

That the eighteen were strangers to police files only reinforced in Henry Barrett Chamberlin's mind something he had learned during the drive on the first group of public enemies: the Chicago police could not be relied upon in the war against Chicago gangsters. Still, Chamberlin remained optimistic. If his public enemies drive had achieved nothing else, it had galvanized public opinion against Public Enemy Number One. "An indifferent public has permitted Capone to prosper for ten years," said Chamberlin. "An aroused public sentiment will bring about his downfall."[76]

8

The Mystery
of the Secret Six

At noon on February 5, 1930, a black sedan stopped at the curb in front of a new hospital under construction at the University of Chicago. Two men stepped out of the car.

"Meagher here?" they asked a workman.

"Sure—that's him over there."

The strangers walked up to the foreman, calmly drew revolvers from their overcoat pockets, riddled the man with bullets, climbed back into the sedan, and drove off. It was one of those unpleasant little episodes that broke the monotony between lunch and supper in Chicago during the roaring twenties. Substantially the same sort of thing had happened time and again. But this time the situation contained two new elements. One was Colonel Robert Isham Randolph.

In the previous December, Randolph had been elected president of the Chicago Association of Commerce—not with any idea that he might direct a fight against crime, but because he seemed a good man for the honorary post. Then the contractor who was Meagher's boss came to see him. Here was the second element: the contractor's insight and arguments. He said:

> My partner and I believe this shooting is the beginning of war. The first signal that the gangs are muscling in on us and mean to have a piece of the pie. If they're given half a chance, they won't let up till every contractor in Chicago is tossing a divvy into the pot.
> What will that do to building costs and employment? Seventy-five percent of the contractors are members of the Association of Commerce. What's the association going to do?[1]

If he had been that kind of fellow, the colonel might have shrugged his shoulders and said: "Sorry, but we can't do anything. A police job. Leave it to the police."

Randolph didn't say that. Any streetwise child in Chicago could tell exactly how far the police would have gotten. Randolph thirsted for direct action. The old vigilante impulse arose—to do something that would leave no doubt in anybody's mind that someone was on the job and meant business. The situation, he felt, called for a figurative corpse at the noose end of a rope. He discussed it with the executive committee of the association. They agreed. State's Attorney Swanson, present by invitation, told what might be accomplished by expert investigators who could work in absolute secrecy—as the state's men and women could not because their names appeared on a public payroll.

A day later Randolph lunched quietly at the Mid-Day Club with a chosen handful of the richest and most influential men in Chicago.

"I don't see any great harm done," said one of the group frankly. "Let 'em kill each other off. Just so they don't touch decent citizens."

So it went. Until finally one, who was the richest and most influential in the group, impatient at drift and indifference, said:

"I can't stay here forever. I'm going, Colonel. I'll leave this on the table; put me down for 10 percent of any amount you raise."

That decided it. The others subscribed like woolly lambs.

These men, with no gift for self-dramatization, organized loosely under Randolph's chairmanship, calling themselves the Citizens Committee for the Prevention and Punishment of Crime. Along came a reporter seeking information about the committee. When Randolph refused to reveal the names of committee members, the reporter christened the group "The Secret Six." From that minute the success of the venture was assured. Gangsters might thumb their noses at a citizens' committee, but "Secret Six," with all that the name portended, was a gun of a different caliber. It sounded like night riders and sudden death—and nothing to catch hold of but shadows.[2]

Gearing Up for Battle

To finance a private venture in crime fighting, Randolph solicited money from Chicago's wealthiest citizens. It was not a brass-band job. This precaution was well justified. Most persons of wealth and public spirit were afraid of Capone so Randolph saw them quietly and personally.

Randolph collected a total of one million dollars to fight crime in

Chicago.[3] One businessman gave $35,000, and four donated $25,000 each. The generous response to this private appeal reflected a strong Chicago spirit. Having adequate funds proved to be a great source of strength; little could have been accomplished if the Secret Six had been without financial resources.

After organizing a committee to receive and disburse the funds subscribed by secret donors, Randolph linked the Secret Six to a number of existing agencies that had already done work on Chicago's crime problem. The Employers' Association had been organized to fight labor rackets and the criminal element that made a business of preying upon union labor organizations and employers of union labor. It had done effective work in its field and had one outstanding asset— Walter Walker, a young man who had been an assistant state's attorney and possessed a knack for detective work. Walker had built up a small but capable force of investigators who knew their tenure of service was independent of political pull. They had the comfortable assurance that their identities were not exposed by spreading their names on a public payroll.

Inevitably, the Prohibition unit for the Chicago federal district became an important element in the network of agencies with which the Secret Six forged ties. The Secret Six also had the cooperation of the U.S. Secret Service and of the U.S. district attorney of Chicago. Federal cooperation became immensely important to the Secret Six. The Secret Six also became useful to federal law enforcers, for the Six had money that Randolph could use at any instant, at his discretion, without the unwinding of red tape with which governmental funds were protected.[4]

Of course, booze was the big racket, the backbone of gang crime in Chicago. The specific objective of the Secret Six was not the enforcement of the Prohibition laws but the reduction of crime in Chicago, particularly homicides and other crimes of violence. However, the big booty attached to the booze racket inspired a constant feudal warfare between rival gangs and greatly raised Chicago's homicide rate. Since the largest armies of killers were enlisted in the booze forces, it followed that convictions under the Prohibition laws seemed to offer the best means of reducing murder. Hence, the Secret Six worked closely with the federal Prohibition law enforcement agencies.

Another existing agency that contributed to usefulness of the Secret

Six's efforts was the Chicago Crime Commission. Its greatest work had been that of compiling two public enemies' lists. In addition, the Commission was the only existing source of continuous criminal records available in Chicago or the state of Illinois. Whenever the Secret Six required accurate information on crime trends in Chicago, it relied on the Crime Commission.

"The Ends Justify the Means"

Public distrust of the police revealed itself almost daily in complaints about the police and crime that citizens made to the Secret Six. When the Secret Six responded to such information, their intention was "to get results" rather than to make a show for the public. Therefore, most of the cases in which the Secret Six participated were unknown to the public. Occasionally, however, an accident or a tragedy disclosed the operations of the Secret Six. Randolph told this tale of a midnight ambush:

> One of the best undercover men on the state's attorney's staff was killed in the raiding of a beer flat run by an ex-policeman who had decided that he could make a fortune more quickly in gang activities than on the police department payroll. Luck seemed to be with him for a time. Somehow he contrived to secure and dispose of a valuable diamond ring. Apparently some of his associates were dissatisfied with the transaction. Anyhow, one day the ex-policeman returned home with three knife wounds in his abdomen. This was not the first time he had been in trouble with the gang. Once before, his place had been raided by hoodlums, who had relieved him of $2,000. Evidently the ex-policeman was considered a poor divider—a trait which may have been a hang-over from his police experience.
>
> We received word from one of our undercover men that the ex-policemen was due to receive a visit at midnight. As he was in bed from his knife wounds, he was glad to get any help available. We planted four men in the flat and awaited the invaders, who arrived on schedule; two at the back door and two at the front. They ordered the ex-policeman's wife to take them to her husband. The instant they were inside the house our men emerged from their hiding places and the battle began. When the smoke cleared away, the ex-police officer was dead in his bed, two of the gangsters were dead, one of our men was mortally wounded, and two other gangsters were wounded, but got away.[5]

Randolph's credo for crime fighting was "the ends justify the means." As he put it, "we will try anything which will put the gangster behind bars." He neutralized the law as a restraint over the Secret Six, using the traditional rationalization for vigilantism—namely, that private action was necessary because law and order had broken down.

Randolph's dicta indicate he had little regard for due process of law.

1. Continued questioning by relays of inquisitors who keep the victim awake and permit him no rest may be regarded as mental torture, but I cannot believe that an innocent man could not support such an ordeal or be made to confess anything but the truth.

2. What constitutional guarantees, code of ethics, or principles of justice would be violated if by any method a confession could be wrung from the kidnapers and murders of the Lindbergh baby?

3. No honest man needs to defend his liberties nowadays; constitutional rights are invoked only as evasions and loopholes to escape the law.

4. A refusal to testify shows guilt.[6]

It never dawned on Randolph that someday he might find himself in a situation where it became necessary to plead the Fifth Amendment. According to Randolph, law enforcers and their agents should be allowed to use any means available to wring confessions out of suspects. Randolph conceded that "we do not hire the best brains in the country to do our police work, but none of them is so stupid as to mark or maim a prisoner so that evidence of his mistreatment may be produced to defend a guilty man." He noted that the fist, the rubber hose, or any other weapon would be too likely to leave its mark. "In the hands of a strong man a telephone book can knock a victim silly and not leave a mark," Randolph said.[7]

Secret Six: Myth or Reality?

In Randolph's first public statement concerning the Secret Six, he took a direct fling at the Cook County state's attorney and the Chicago police. He referred to "hundreds of indictments in which there have been no subsequent convictions; a great number of felonies committed and followed by no arrests; and the total failure to stop bombings." Mentioning the murder of Meagher, he announced that the Association of Commerce was offering a $5,000 reward for the arrest and conviction of the two men who shot Meagher. He issued an ultimatum: "Gang rule, gang violence, gang crime of every kind, must be stopped: and if it is not stopped at once by the authorities, then it will be stopped by the citizens of Chicago themselves."[8]

Spurred on by Randolph's criticism, twenty-five detectives attended the prizefights at the Chicago Coliseum on tickets paid for by Police Commissioner Russell. At the close of the fights on February 8, detectives picked up seven men with criminal records. Yet, the Loop saloons and the Loop handbooks and the Loop brothels—the financial backbone of the Capone syndicate—continued to operate in high gear.

"Hymie" Levine, collector for the Capone beer syndicate, accompanied by two henchmen, made the rounds of Loop speakeasies collecting the beer money. Levine greeted affably all policemen he encountered in the saloons. The policemen, apparently unaffected by the new drive on crime, failed to pick up "Hymie" and neglected to search his armed bodyguards. Nonetheless, the official word from the police department to the Association of Commerce was that law enforcement authorities were keeping a constant check on the beer in the Loop. It worked like this:

Two plainclothesmen would enter a speakeasy. "Gotta have a sample of your beer," one of the undercover cops would say. "The boss wants it."

"Sure," the barkeep would reply. "What'll you have while I'm drawing it?"

"Oh, give us a shot."

So the bartender would pour shots for the law enforcers. Then he would go to the near-beer tap, draw a bottle of near beer, and hand the bottle of beer to the policemen. After downing the shots, the cops would confiscate the beer and take it to their captain to assure him that only near beer was being served. Official pronouncements that only near beer was being sold in the Loop resulted from this sort of hocus-pocus on the part of authorities.

As for the handbooks, they were operating with little concealment. Racing sheets adorned the walls in many of the handbooks, and in many more the staccato voice of the broadcaster could be heard calling the race at the quarter, the half, and in the stretch. One handbook had made its customary donation to the police just before the Association of Commerce's drive on crime began. The policemen appeared somewhat embarrassed at this turn of events and their advice was: "Be reasonable. Only let in a few guys at a time and don't let in anybody you don't know. We're having a big stirrup and we don't want things too wide open."[9]

Unimpressed by the counterfeit response of the police, Randolph sought to boost police morale. On April 3, the Secret Six sponsored a banquet for Chicago's law enforcers in the grand ballroom of the LaSalle Hotel. Chief of Detectives Stege and thirty police officers represented the Chicago Police Department; District Attorney George E. Q. Johnson represented the federal forces; and State's Attorney Swanson and his assistant, C. Wayland Brooks, came on behalf of the county forces. Colonel Randolph was there, too, and seated among the more than a thousand businessmen were the other members of the Secret Six. Cooperation was the theme of the banquet. Criminal justice authorities said they were doing their best and urged support of the businessmen. The businessmen, through their spokesperson Colonel Randolph, made it plain that the authorities had the moral and financial backing of business.

Randolph introduced Jerry Bowen and James O'Neill as examples of the thirty police heroes who sat at the speakers' table. Colonel Randolph stated that each had been shot three times in getting "his man." When Bowen, a black man, arose, the businessmen registered their approval with loud applause. Colonel Randolph then introduced State's Attorney Swanson, referring to him as "the man who was dynamited into office."[10]

Aside from the delegation of police heroes who attended the banquet, local law enforcement officials gave a chilly reception to the Secret Six. When questioned by a *Toronto Star* reporter about the Secret Six, Police Commissioner William Russell roared, "The Secret Six is all a myth; it's newspaper bologna."

Less emphatic about the nonexistence of the Six, Chief of Detectives John Stege said: "We have never heard a thing about it. We don't know what it is all about."

Later on, when the same reporter passed on to Randolph what Russell and Stege had said about the Six, Randolph didn't say a thing. He simply stared at the reporter and smiled. According to the reporter, Randolph's smile "was the most informative thing Randolph said in the interview." In describing Randolph's smile, the reporter wrote:

"Colonel Randolph's smile is exactly the kind that Bugs Moran and Scarface Al see in their nightmares. Across their path is a foreboding shadow, cast by a secret organization in the interest of law and order. And behind that secret organization is the cryptic, deranging smile of Colonel Robert Isham Randolph."[11]

Alexander G. Jamie

Randolph picked as operating director of the Secret Six a man renowned for his incorruptibility. This man had extensive experience in intelligence gathering and criminal investigations, possessed detailed knowledge of the underworld in Chicago, and carried with him the endorsement of the president of the United States. At the time of the formation of the Secret Six, he was the chief special agent of the Prohibition Bureau in Chicago. Randolph had to go to President Hoover to get a leave of absence for the Prohibition agent. After persuading President Hoover to lend Alexander G. Jamie to the Secret Six, Randolph named him director of the Secret Six.[12]

Unlike his brother-in-law Eliot Ness, Alexander Jamie was never accused of being a glory-seeker; his style was to bow out after accomplishing something and allow others to take credit for his work.[13] In one of the few cases Jamie received the credit due him, he led special Prohibition agents on raids of two of Ralph Capone's Cicero nightclubs, the Cotton Club at 5240 22nd Street and the Greyhound Inn, on May 8, 1930. Those raids were part of a much larger investigation focusing on Ralph Capone's leadership of a liquor smuggling business in which two large cabin airplanes were used to run more than $1,000,000 worth of whiskey from Windsor, Ontario, to Cicero. The planes were flown into Cicero with the approach of darkness, one of them circling above the landing field while the other landed. The contraband would be eased to the ground through a sliding door in the fuselage, and the empty plane would then take to the air and circle above while the other plane came down to unload. Trucks driven by Capone henchmen waited at the field to pick up the whiskey brought by the planes. Old Smuggler and Johnny Walker Scotch whiskeys and various brands of bourbon were smuggled in. The value of the liquor was $50 a case in Canada and $100 a case in Chicago. On the basis of six flights a week, the planes made 200 flights in more than eight months of operation. With seventy cases brought in on each trip, this would be 14,000 cases with a bootleg value of $1,400,000.[14] Following Jamie's investigation, a federal grand jury returned 100 indictments, charging Ralph Capone and 200 others with liquor violations.

After joining the Secret Six, Jamie put together an organizational chart of the Capone syndicate. In Jamie's view, Al Capone modeled his gang along the lines of modern big business. Capone, as dictator, had as his two aides a powerful labor racketeer in Chicago and an ex-convict. The latter might properly be called a field marshal. Next came the "board of strategy," corresponding to a board of directors. They were gang lieutenants, each in charge of a particular branch of the enterprise. A member of that board also served as business manager of the syndicate. Next in line came the "fixer" who dealt with policemen and other public officials who were willing to "listen to common sense"; the "supervisor" made certain that orders of the business manager were carried out; and a "traffic manager" attended to liquor deliveries of beer and liquor from Capone breweries and alcohol plants to speakeasies.

The rest of the organization was divided into departments, each run by a department head. The alcohol division controlled the production and distribution of all syndicate alcohol; the beer division regulated the manufacture, sale, and delivery of beer to the thousands of speakeasies in Chicago and vicinity; the buildings division procured suitable locations for breweries, distilleries, and alky-cooking plants; the collections division interlocked closely with all revenue-producing departments and collected tribute from former independent gangs who were forced to make regular payments to the Capone syndicate; the gambling division supervised gambling houses, slot machines, and thousands of the larger racetrack booking establishments in Chicago; the vice division controlled many of the larger houses of prostitution within a 200-mile radius of Chicago; and the enforcement division handled bombings, killings, and terroristic threats.

How to Wreck the Capone Gang

Robert Isham Randolph made a prophecy: The legalization of 4 percent beer would wreck the criminal gangs whose murders, extortions, and briberies have been so spectacular as to give Chicago its reputation for lawlessness.[15] He advocated the repeal of Prohibition.[16]

To support his position, Randolph cited estimates of the bootleg-ging business made in a survey by Secret Six investigators. Figures set down by Secret Six operatives were for Cook County, which was generally identical with Chicago, since, of the county's 3,900,000 in-habitants, more than 3,300,000 lived in the city. In Cook County, Secret Six operatives found 20,000 beer joints, places that varied in size from large soft-drink parlors, saloons, and night clubs to beer flats, assignation houses, cafes, and dark rooms in the rear of tobacco shops and poolrooms. In Chicago's Loop alone investigators found 160 spots. Whiskey and gin were included in the stock of such speak-easies, but beer was the staple commodity. It sold at the standard rate of one dollar a bottle or twenty-five cents a glass.

According to the Secret Six's survey, those 20,000 spots were served with beer by professional bootleggers, the bulk of whom belonged to the Capone syndicate. Smaller beer-running gangs flourishing in smaller areas of the city paid Capone tribute for the privilege. Capone's syndicate controlled the illicit business of bootlegging from manufac-ture to distribution. It owned a string of breweries and controlled the output of many others, operating them periodically or constantly, depending upon how often the law enforcers were bribed. Secret Six investigators estimated the 20,000 spots averaged 5 barrels per week, which meant that the syndicate profited from the making and handling of 100,000 barrels of beer every seven days. In other words, Cook County's normal consumption of beer was about 25,000,000 pints a week. That came to over 6 pints per inhabitant.

Most of this was sold in bulk, hauled from brewery to speakeasy in barrels by the truckload. Much of it was bottled in syndicate plants where it could be labeled "Canadian Ale." Usually the syndicate kept up a pretense that the draft beer delivered in barrels was only near beer, but even the policemen on their beats laughed at that notion.

The Secret Six's investigation showed that it cost Capone $1.80 to brew a barrel of beer and that other manufacturing charges, such as cooperage, brought the total to more than $3. Now the standard price charged speakeasies for the same barrel was $55, leaving a gross profit of $52. The least of the expense of distribution was trucking. The highest item was protection. The armed guards who accompanied the trucks and the gunmen who collected from the proprietors of the speakeasies could be had by Capone for $100 to $150 a week. Higher salaried gangsters were needed to "fix" the police, and still more intelligent operators were used to "see" the right politicians.

The closest estimate Secret Six investigators could make as to the number of men on Capone's payroll was 2,000, counting the brewers, truckmen, armed guards, collectors, fixers, and custodians of brothels, gambling houses, and handbooks that Capone's syndicate directly owned. This did not include the vice population that paid Capone tribute. It did not include the more than half of Chicago's 6,000 police officers who took bribes spasmodically or regularly from Capone.[17]

Direct Action

Even though logic and facts supported legalizing liquor, Randolph sensed that the national political climate was not right in 1931 for repealing "the noble experiment." Something had to be done about Capone, and Randolph could not wait for the public to see that Prohibition was nonsense as a crime policy. Working quietly behind the scenes, Randolph promoted the idea of a special task force of Justice Department agents who would raid Capone's breweries, tap his telephones, and spy on his operations.[18] He proposed the idea of a special unit to U.S. District Attorney George E. Q. Johnson and even recommended to Johnson a man who could lead such a unit into battle. That man was Alexander Jamie's brother-in-law Eliot Ness.

Along with his "Untouchables," Ness tapped the telephone in Ralph Capone's headquarters at the Montmartre Cafe, a plush speakeasy in Cicero. That wiretap enabled the Untouchables to discover where the Capone's gang's breweries were located. The Ness team, driving a ten-ton truck with a flatbed to support scaling ladders and a steel bumper that covered the whole radiator, battered down doors of nineteen Capone distilleries and six breweries, and seized or destroyed more than $1 million worth of trucks, equipment, beer, and whiskey.[19]

To further disrupt Capone's business, Randolph opened a speakeasy "to play with the bootleggers."[20] Playing with the bootleggers translated into buying information from them about Al Capone and members of his gang. Randolph located the speakeasy deep in Capone territory at 60 East 30th Street. Known as the Garage Cafe, its premises were fitted like a real joint at the cost of $12,000, and beer and liquor were sold there in violation of Prohibition law. Randolph hired Sam Constantino, a Sicilian, and Pat Horan, an undercover policeman with the Chicago Police Department, to tend bar at the speakeasy. Constantino (alias Galgano), who was later sentenced to three months for fraud and seven years for running an interstate stolen goods ring, was working as an informant for the Chicago police.[21]

At the Garage Cafe, Secret Six operatives purchased information from low-ranking members of the Capone gang. Depending on the nature of the information and the reliability of the source, the going rate of pay ranged from $100 to $1,000. The Secret Six operated the speakeasy for six months but were forced to close it when the Sicilian bartender came to Randolph and said, "I'm takin' it on the lam. Here's the keys and I'm goin' and goin' for good." Someone tipped off the Capone gang, and Constantino was leaving before the gang "took him for a ride."[22]

Upon learning through the gangland grapevine about the Secret Six's speakeasy, Al Capone wanted to find out more about the Secret Six. Jake Guzik, Al Capone's right-hand man, telephoned Robert Isham Randolph one night in February 1931 to inform Randolph that Capone, known in the underworld as "The Big Fellow," wanted to meet with him. "I have the Big Fellow planted in a hotel near the Loop where you can talk to him without being seen. Will you go?" asked Guzik.

That night Randolph met with Capone at the Lexington Hotel. Capone offered to end the gang killings that were giving Chicago a bad name if Randolph would persuade District Attorney Johnson's special unit to quit busting up Capone's booze business. After drinking two of his host's beers, Randolph politely declined Capone's offer. At the close of the meeting, Capone asked Randolph whether he should back Thompson or Cermak in the mayoral election of 1931.

Dabbling in Politics

Capone's question about which mayoral candidate to support caused Randolph to examine the alleged ties between Capone and Thompson. From talking with Henry Barrett Chamberlin of the Crime Commission and others, Randolph learned that Daniel Serritella,

Mayor Thompson's city sealer, and other associates of Capone's were influential parts of "Big Bill" Thompson's administration. This convinced Randolph that the Secret Six needed to enter politics.

Urging businessmen to use the ballot "to clean up Chicago for the 1933 World's Fair," Colonel Randolph called upon businessmen to unite regardless of party to guarantee Thompson's defeat in the mayoral election in April 1931. Speaking before the Kiwanis Club on July 28, 1930, Colonel Randolph called upon businessmen to "clean house from the top down, beginning with the politicians who fix things for lawbreakers."[23] Sounding a note of optimism, Randolph said, "Much remains in the hands of voters, now that the Secret Six and the Crime Commission have thrown the light of publicity upon illegal enterprises."

Randolph spiked rumors in November 1930 that he would be a candidate for the Republican nomination as mayor of Chicago. "Not only do I not want to be mayor of Chicago, I can't be mayor of that city because my home is in Riverside," Randolph told a reporter for the *Daily News*.

"But you're interested in who the next mayor is, aren't you?" asked the reporter.

"It's high time all persons living in and around Chicago became interested in the choice of a mayor," replied Randolph.

"What sort of man do you think he should be?"

"Well, in the first place the mayor must be a man who will smash the corrupt alliance between crime and civil government."

"Would a businessman make an ideal mayor?"

"No. The average businessman doesn't know what precinct, ward, congressional or senatorial district he lives in. He doesn't know his committeeman, alderman, congressman or other representative. If he were as blank on his private as he is on his public interests, he would be on the slippery slope to insolvency."

"Colonel Randolph, do you set a high value upon moral excellence in candidates for public office?"

"It is the fundamental value in men. Without moral excellence, a man may glitter in a thousand ways and be only darkness. The new mayor of Chicago should have, before all else, moral excellence. He should be a God-fearing man with a private life above reproach, and a public life without stain."[24]

Randolph joined other Chicago business leaders in urging the energetic coroner, Herman N. Bundesen, to stay out of the mayoral race. Speaking on behalf of Chicago's business interests, with an eye to civic welfare, Randolph warned Bundesen not to split the anti-Thompson vote. Bundesen took Randolph's advice and withdrew on March 3.[25]

Randolph sent Bundesen this note:

My dear Dr. Bundesen:

Permit me to express my appreciation of your wisdom in withdrawing from the mayoralty campaign. Your action has left the issue of the campaign clearly defined. It has enabled those who are opposed to William Hale Thompson to register their opposition effectively by voting for the Democratic candidate. You have done a real service to your city.

With warmest personal regards,

Robert Isham Randolph[26]

Coming on the heels of Bundesen's withdrawal, there followed a jolt of bad luck for Thompson. Under orders from the state's attorney, police raiders entered city hall and seized cabinets of records from the office of Daniel Serritella, Thompson's city sealer. After examination of them by a grand jury, indictments were issued against Serritella—an associate of Capone—and his chief deputy, Harry Hockstein, a personal friend of Frank ("The Enforcer") Nitti. Both were charged with conspiracy to appropriate funds collected for Christmas distribution to the poor. Although a jury found them guilty, an appellate court reversed the decision on the ground that evidence did not establish guilt beyond a reasonable doubt. Serritella and Hockstein escaped the consequences of their behavior, but Thompson did not. He was too closely tied to the Capone gang to avoid implication in the scandal. It helped to make up the electorate's mind.[27]

Anton Cermak swamped "Big Bill" Thompson in the April seventh election, winning forty-five out of Chicago's fifty wards and beginning the Democratic domination of city government. Thompson was trounced thoroughly: he carried only the three wards in the Black Belt and the two where gangster influence was strongest—the bloody Twentieth and the Twenty-eighth, another west side bailiwick of organized crime.

Robert Isham Randolph proclaimed to the press that Chicago, by electing Cermak, had "redeemed itself." "We've had enough of Nero fiddling while Rome burned," said the leader of the Secret Six. "We have told the world that we are prepared to regain our business level and restore our good name."[28]

Silent Partner

At the same time the Untouchables were busting up Capone's breweries and Cermak was defeating Mayor Thompson, the Secret Six were at work on their biggest case. The Six acted as a silent partner to the U.S. Treasury Department in its investigation of Al Capone for tax evasion.

Elmer Irey, the head of the Treasury Department's intelligence unit, was in charge of the Capone investigation. Assisting him were agents Frank Wilson and Pat O'Rourke. Wilson, a genius for detail, later became head of the U.S. Secret Service. O'Rourke was an Irishman who looked like an Italian, and he specialized in undercover investigations.[29] With Secret Six money, O'Rourke purchased gaudy clothes like the gangsters wore: a white hat with a snap brim, several purple shirts, and checked suits. To infiltrate the Capone gang, O'Rourke spent more Secret Six money to rent a room at the Lexington Hotel. After signing the register "Michael Lepito," O'Rourke loitered. He sat reading newspapers or losing Secret Six money to Capone's henchmen while playing the "Fourteen Game," a form of larceny with dice.[30]

For his part, Frank Wilson gathered records from gambling joints, whorehouses, breweries, and other illegal enterprises then operating in Chicago. Local law enforcement agencies had seized these books in raids on gangster joints through the years.

One weekend early in 1930, Wilson reported to his superior Irey: "I think we've got Nitti and Guzik." Frank ("The Enforcer") Nitti was in charge of keeping discipline within the mob, and Jake Guzik provided the "brains" behind Capone.

Wilson continued:

> I know where Al gets his money, but it'll take a little proving. I can prove where Nitti gets his, and how much. The same goes for Guzik. I think we should get them first and then go for Al. Nobody wants to talk much about Al, so maybe if we put a couple of his big-shots away people will be more cooperative.[31]

Wilson's prediction proved accurate. Frank Nitti had erred in endorsing a check for $1,000, which Wilson knew was part of the receipts of a Cicero gambling house. The March 1930 federal grand jury in Chicago handed down a secret indictment charging Nitti with accumulating $742,887.81 in 1925, 1926, and 1927 without paying any taxes. Nitti went "on the lam."

Nailing Guzik

With Nitti unavailable, the intelligence unit concentrated on Guzik. Like Nitti—but unlike Al Capone—Guzik had signed a few checks and was drawing profits from gambling houses. Those profits were deposited under a variety of aliases and withdrawn in the form of cashier's checks. Agents of the intelligence unit knew from handwriting experts that Fred Ries, the cashier at a Capone gambling joint called the Ship, had been depositing and withdrawing the money. They also knew that the withdrawals were being handed over to Guzik.[32]

Wilson tracked down Ries in St. Louis and questioned Ries about his jobs in gambling joints. At first, Ries refused to cooperate, but on September 18, 1930, he agreed to testify against Guzik, Nitti, and Al Capone. Ries explained the structure of the Capone organization and asserted that more than half of the profits from the Capone's gang's gambling establishments went into the pockets of Al Capone himself.[33] After coaxing this information out of Ries, Wilson took him to downstate Danville, where Ries was locked up in jail for safekeeping.

Guzik's trial began on November 12. The federal government charged him with attempts to defraud the government of more than $200,000 in taxes on a total income of $1,043,144 for 1927, 1928, and 1929.[34] When the government's star witness testified on November 14, it presented the spectacle of a Capone gambler "putting the finger" on one of the "big shots" of his gang and disclosing the enormous profits of the gambling enterprises of the syndicate. Ries, a middle-aged man, bald, and wearing horned-rimmed glasses, told how the gambling houses run by Guzik in Cicero would receive frequent "orders to move" and how another place would be waiting a few doors or a few blocks away. He named the stands of the circulating "house" as the Ship, 2127 South Cicero Avenue; the Subway, 4738 West 22nd

Street; Lauderbach's, 12th Street and 46th Court; the Radio, in the 4500 block of West 23rd Street; the Garage, 50th Avenue and 25th Street; and the storeroom in the Western Hotel. Ries explained that during 1927 and 1928 he worked for Guzik as general cashier, in charge of all the money for the horserace betting and the blackjack, chuck-a-luck, roulette, and craps tables.

U.S. Attorney Dwight H. Green questioned Ries, eliciting information showing that the average monthly net profit of a Capone-owned gambling house was $30,000. The testimony also brought out that Ries used profits from gambling to purchase cashier's checks which, in turn, he gave to Guzik's chauffeur. During the examination of other witnesses, Green traced the same cashier's checks to Guzik's account in the Equitable Trust Company.[35] A jury found Guzik guilty on three counts of evading income tax. The judge sentenced him to fifteen years in Leavenworth penitentiary and fined him $20,000.

Protecting Ries, Catching Nitti, Spying on Capone

With Guzik's conviction emerged an obstacle standing in the way of the Treasury agents. Ries possessed a great deal of information needed to make a case against Al Capone. If the agents jailed Ries again, they would have a hostile witness in future cases. If they freed him, they would have a dead witness. At that time the federal government lacked a program to protect witnesses, so the intelligence unit agents had to find a way to safeguard Ries until Al Capone's trial.

To cover the costs of harboring Ries, the Six gave $10,000 to the Treasury Department. Using Secret Six money, Wilson sent Ries to New Orleans, where Ries boarded a steamer headed for South America. Ries spent ninety days on an ocean voyage, returning for Al Capone's trial in October 1931.[36]

While Ries was sailing the Atlantic, a federal grand jury indicted Nitti for income tax evasion. If the tax investigators could apprehend Nitti, the way would be cleared for making a case against Al Capone. Once again, the Secret Six assisted. A private detective employed by the Secret Six paid a low-ranking member of the Capone gang $1,000 for information that Nitti was hiding in a bungalow in Berwyn, Illinois, a western suburb of Chicago.[37] Secret Six detectives rented houses on two sides of the bungalow and watched for signs of Nitti. One night

Nitti neglected to draw the shades when he went into the kitchen for a cold bottle of beer. The private sleuths recognized him, went next door, and took him into custody.[38] On December 20, Nitti pleaded guilty to charges of evading $153,323 in federal income taxes. He was sentenced to eighteen months in Leavenworth penitentiary and fined $10,000.[39]

With the conviction of Nitti, agents of the Internal Revenue Bureau began digging up information on the extent of Capone's expenditures. O'Rourke spent Secret Six money in traveling with Capone's men to Florida, where Capone was in residence at his estate on Palm Island. While there, O'Rourke observed the sixty-foot yacht moored at the back of the Capone mansion and the semipublic gambling house on Palm Island, which Capone ran. O'Rourke also acquired evidence showing that Capone's bill for household supplies and for beer, wine, liquor, and fancy liqueurs smuggled in from the Bahamas was $4,000 a week. Armed with this information about expenditures in Florida, O'Rourke returned to Chicago, where he obtained from department stores further evidence of Capone's luxury spending for items such as silk underwear and diamond-studded belt buckles.[40]

That evidence only proved that Capone had money and was spending it. What was needed now was information on Capone's income. In conferences between Capone's attorney and Wilson, the attorney conceded that his client's enterprises had produced income. When Wilson asked him to state how much in writing, Capone's lawyer stipulated that Capone received one-sixth of the profits from "an illegal" organization; that Capone had never made over $75 a week until 1926; and that Capone had never made more than $100,000 in one year.[41]

The Invisible Hand

Wilson set out to discover the amount Capone was receiving one-sixth of and to see if Capone was receiving an even greater share. One evening Wilson found a ledger picked up in previous raids that bore the title, "Barracks, Burnham, Ill." Wilson knew the Barracks was an old Capone bagnio so he opened the book. In a moment he realized that it was not a ledger for a red-light place. The entries showed it to be the record for a gambling dive dealing in horses, dice, birdcage, and roulette.[42]

These words grabbed Wilson's attention: "Frank paid $17,500 for Al." As he skimmed through the book, Wilson found other mentions of Al. He noticed that every month the profits were divided, with the biggest shares set aside for "Town." Wilson knew "Town" referred to graft paid to city officials.[43] To prove that the references to "Al" meant Al Capone, Wilson would have to locate the man who had made the entries. And to do that he would have to find out what gambling joint the erroneously titled book covered. Police identified the book as having been confiscated in a raid on the Hawthorne Smoke Shop, a Capone gambling joint in Cicero. The raid had been made on April 26, 1926, the day William McSwiggin, an assistant state's attorney, had been murdered.

Wilson found out that Leslie Shumway had been the bookkeeper at the Hawthorne. That Shumway was in hiding came as no surprise to Wilson, who located him in Miami. In February 1931, four months after he had been identified as the keeper of the Smoke Shop's books, Shumway met with Wilson and figured out the profits of the Smoke Shop.[44] In the twenty-two months Shumway had worked there, between 1924 and 1926, the place had cleared $587,721.95. Even if Capone received only the one-sixth he had already confessed to, he made $97,970.33 from the Smoke Shop alone in a period when he reported his income had at no time exceeded $75 a week.

Wilson spirited Shumway out of Miami, bringing him to Chicago in secrecy. Shumway testified before a secret grand jury, which charged Al Capone on March 13, 1931, with evading income taxes for 1924. The indictment was kept secret at the government's request while Shumway left for California accompanied by an agent of the intelligence unit. Again the invisible hand of the Secret Six reached out to assist federal law enforcers. To hide Shumway until Capone's trial, agents of the intelligence unit once again relied upon Secret Six money.[45]

On June 5 a federal grand jury indicted Al Capone on twenty-two counts charging tax evasion for 1925 through 1929. Those charges plus the March jury's indictment resulted in a bill against Capone for $215,030.48 in unpaid taxes. Three hours after the second indictment was returned, Capone gave himself up, and in about a half hour he was free on $50,000 bail. A week later the grand jury returned a third indictment. This one, based on evidence gathered by Eliot Ness and his Prohibition agents, charged Capone and sixty-eight members of his gang with conspiring to violate the Volstead Act. Five thousand offenses were listed, four thousand of them involving beer truck deliveries.[46]

Back at the Lexington, the invisible hand was again silently at work. O'Rourke, the T-man whose undercover mission was being financed by Secret Six money, heard that Capone had imported five hoodlums from New York to shoot Frank Wilson, Arthur P. Madden (the agent in charge of the intelligence unit in Chicago), George E. Q. Johnson, and Pat Roche in hopes that this demonstration of firepower would deter the authorities from continuing with the prosecution or, at least, from voting him guilty. That tip caused the agents to change hotels and take other precautionary measures that may have saved their lives.

Capone's second strategy was now tried. Negotiations took place. Unofficial approaches were made to government representatives by Capone's attorneys, suggesting a deal. On June 16, Capone appeared before Judge James H. Wilkerson and pled guilty to tax evasion and to 5,000 Prohibition charges in exchange for what Capone thought would be a two-and-a-half-year jail sentence. But on July 30, Judge Wilkerson refused to honor the plea bargain, and so Capone's counsel withdrew the guilty pleas. Capone would have to stand trial. He would be tried only on the income tax charges because Judge Wilkerson determined they took precedence over the Prohibition charges.

The Trial

Even though Robert Isham Randolph played no official part in Al Capone's trial, the Secret Six helped determine the outcome. If the Secret Six had not made arrangements for the protection of the government's two key witnesses, Shumway and Ries, they might have been "taken for a ride." Losing Shumway and Ries would have almost certainly spoiled the government's chances of convicting Capone.

Assistant U.S. Attorney Dwight Green made the opening statement for the government at Capone's trial on October 6. Green explained the consolidated indictments alleging Capone had failed to pay any tax on big incomes for the years 1924 to 1929. The government charged Capone with evasion of $215,000 in taxes on a total income of $1,038,654 during the six years. Albert Fink, speaking for the defense, waived an opening statement, and Green commenced direct examination of the prosecution's witnesses.

Charles W. Arndt, chief of the Income Tax Division of the Internal Revenue Bureau of the Chicago district, testified that Capone filed no returns for the years 1924–1929; Chester Bragg, an insurance agent, informed the jury that Capone had told him that he owned a gambling hall in Cicero; and the Reverend Henry C. Hoover, an earnest young suburban pastor, corroborated Bragg's testimony.

Leslie Shumway, the onetime Hawthorne Smoke Shop betting agent whom the Secret Six had protected, testified on the seventh. Assistant U.S. Attorney Jacob I. Grossman questioned Shumway, a nervous, elderly man, who kept a handkerchief or hand to his mouth and who spoke almost inaudibly.[47]

Shumway gave details of how the Smoke Shop was run, producing a thirty-four-page loose-leaf book containing a series of daily financial reports. Grossman went through the large volume, page by page. Shumway recited tabulations of the profits of the houses during 1924, 1925, and 1926. Through Shumway's testimony, the prosecution showed profits to the houses that Capone owned of $300,250 in 1924, $117,400 in 1925, and $170,011 during four months of 1926.[48]

On the third day of the trial, Capone found himself caught in a net of his own weaving. After an all-day court battle by his attorneys, Judge Wilkerson admitted into evidence a "confession letter," a document in which the chief of Chicago gangland, through his Washington attorney, admitted income as high as $100,000 a year, upon which he paid no tax.[49]

The fourth day featured a host of witnesses for the prosecution who told of Capone's high spending. Those witnesses revealed that while Capone stayed at his Florida mansion he received thousands of dollars in money transfers from Chicago and that Capone made enormous expenditures for food, clothing, homes, and other items. On the fifth, sixth, and seventh days of the trial, the prosecution rushed many more clerks and salespersons through the witness box to add to the mass of evidence about Capone's expenditures.

The final blast of evidence directed by the government against

Capone came from Fred Ries, former cashier in the syndicate's houses in Cicero. When Ries—a tall, thin man, bald, with stony, expressionless eyes behind steel-rimmed glasses—marched to the witness stand, there was a stir in the courtroom. Long sought by the Capone gang for his testimony in the income tax trial of Guzik, Ries had been under the protection of the Secret Six. As assistant U.S. Attorney Grossman began to examine Ries, Capone sat erect and became intent with interest.[50]

> **Grossman:** Were you a cashier at the Subway, a gambling house at 4738 West 22nd Street in Cicero in 1927?
>
> **Ries:** Yes.
>
> **Grossman:** Did you see the defendant there?
>
> **Ries:** Yes, sir.
>
> **Grossman:** What was he doing?
>
> **Ries:** He was in the telegraph operator's office talking to Jack [Jake] Guzik.
>
> **Grossman:** Did you see him in the place you operated known as the Radio?
>
> **Ries:** Yes, I was taking bets at the counter. He came by and said, "Hello, Ries." I said, "Hello, Al."
>
> **Grossman:** What did you do with the profits of the places you operated?
>
> **Ries:** I purchased checks with them and turned them over to Bobby Barton.
>
> **Grossman:** What were the total profits during 1927?
>
> **Ries:** Around $150,000.
>
> **Grossman:** I show you here forty-three cashier's checks. Tell us about them.
>
> **Ries:** They represented profits above the bank roll of $10,000 we always kept and above all expenses which I paid out. I bought the checks and gave them to Bobby Barton.[51]

Grossman read the checks into the record. They were endorsed by J. C. Dunbar, an alias of Fred Ries, and deposited to the credit of the Laramie Kennel Club in the First National Bank of Cicero. The forty-three checks totaled $177,500 for 1927 and $24,800 for 1928. For the end, the Government saved a damning circumstance: a signature, "Al Capone," appeared on the back of one of the checks. A handwriting expert testified that the signature "Al Capone" on a safety deposit contract previously introduced in the trial was the same as that on the check.

The moment Ries left the stand District Attorney Johnson rose and said, "Your honor, at this time the government rests its case."

Capone's defense was that what he had made by gambling he had lost by gambling. Cicero gambling halls may have made money for Capone, but Capone lost it on the races. So the defense counsel called in a crowd of bookmakers who testified that Capone always lost money because he bet on losing horses.[52]

After one day of hearing from gambler-witnesses, the prosecution and defense delivered their closing arguments. Judge Wilkerson instructed the jury for over an hour, and then the twelve jurors retired to their jury room during the middle of the day. At 9:30 P.M. sounds of applause emanated from the jury room. A last juror had been won over.[53]

The Verdict

Fifteen minutes from the time Capone had been notified that a verdict had been reached, he and his attorneys were in court. Capone walked briskly to the center of the courtroom and sat in place at the defense table.

Judge Wilkerson emerged from his chambers and took his seat. "Have you arrived at a verdict?" inquired Judge Wilkerson.

The foreman of the jury nodded and handed a packet of papers, including the verdict, to a bailiff who in turn gave it to the court clerk.

"On indictment number 22,852 (the charges for 1924) we find the defendant not guilty," read the clerk.

Next, Capone heard the clerk say he was "guilty" of tax evasion in 1925. Then, he heard "not guilty" for the next three counts in that same year. It was the same for 1926 and 1927: guilty on the first count for each year; not guilty on the other counts. Strangely, the jury found Capone not guilty of felony tax evasion for 1928 and 1929, but guilty of the misdemeanor counts for those same years.

Capone spoke to his attorneys as they rose to advance to the bench. The gang chief smiled, and later, in the corridors while he was being led to jail, Capone joked and chatted with friends.[54]

Six days later, on October 24, Capone appeared in court again where Judge Wilkerson sentenced him to eleven years in prison and fined him $50,000.[55] While Capone was waiting in jail to be transported to the federal penitentiary in Atlanta, Georgia, a reporter from a Detroit newspaper asked Capone who should receive the credit for bringing him to justice.

"The Secret Six licked the rackets," replied Capone. "They've licked me. They've made it so there's no money in the game anymore."[56]

Those who might question Capone's sincerity in making this statement need only consider what Frank Wilson, the investigator for the Treasury Department, said ten years after Capone's conviction. Wilson wrote this note to Robert Isham Randolph: "The exceptionally valuable assistance which you rendered to me during the period I was engaged on the Capone case is well remembered as it was one of the important factors in our success."[57]

Unraveling the Mystery of the Secret Six

With Capone in prison, the press set out to solve the mystery of the Secret Six. Efforts by Chicago newspaper reporters to discover the identities of the Six flushed a rich assortment of suspects but failed to produce much evidence as to who actually belonged to the clandestine group. Today, sixty-some years after Capone's conviction, six men can be said with certainty to have had a hand in the surreptitious activities of the Secret Six.

U.S. Bureau of Investigation reports indicate that *Julius Rosenwald*, chairman of the board of Sears, Roebuck and Company, and *Frank F. Loesch*, the president of the Chicago Crime Commission, belonged to the Secret Six.[58] In interviews Robert Isham Randolph gave to the press after Capone's conviction, he named Rosenwald and *Samuel Insull* as members and key financial backers of the Secret Six.[59] Judge John H. Lyle, who assisted Henry Barrett Chamberlin in the public enemies drive, identified *Edward E. Gore*, Samuel Insull, and *George A. Paddock*, an Evanston stockbroker, as members of the Secret Six.[60] Minutes of executive committee meetings of the Chicago Crime Commission confirm that Gore attended meetings of the Secret Six.[61] As for the sixth man, *Colonel Randolph* openly declared his membership in the Secret Six in 1931.[62]

9

Whatever Happened to the Crime Crusaders?

"NOW LET US DRIVE OUT ALL THE GANGSTERS!" This clarion call rang out across the front page of the *Chicago American* several days after Capone's conviction. The newspaper exhorted the citizens of Chicago to "get rid of Capone's gang; break up his shameful syndicate of illicit enterprises, of murder and bribery and prostitution; and drive out every member of Capone's gang."[1]

The *Chicago Daily News*, speaking editorially, made a similar plea. It asked: "After Capone, who?" The *News* advised its readers that to destroy gangs it was necessary first to clean up the political situation that made gangs possible and to deprive the gangsters of the benefits of alliances with political machines.[2]

Despite those calls for action, the crusade fizzled out. Business leaders who helped put Capone in prison were not so naive as to think that Capone would not have powerful successors. They realized that the conditions that gave Capone his opportunities would produce other lords of gangdom. They knew the people of the city wanted action and desired the removal of all gang members from Chicago. So what kept them from marching on in pursuit of the remaining gangsters in the city?

An unfortunate diversion, the Great Depression, sidetracked the crime crusaders. During the years 1930–1932, the businessman's worldview—the premise that prosperity and progress would ever grow under laissez-faire capitalism—collapsed with the Big Bull Market. It was the time of the down-and-outers' Hoovervilles built out of packing-cases and corrugated iron on the spare lots of Chicago, the time of soup kitchens and breadlines. No American city had higher unemployment than Chicago. None had a bigger proportion of the working population on relief. In one month in 1932 thirty-eight Chicago banks closed their doors.[3]

During 1930, 1931, and 1932, Chicago tottered on the brink of bankruptcy. At one point Chicago was in debt $300,000,000. In November 1931, one month after Capone had been convicted, the president of the First National Bank of Chicago said: "We are busted in the United States." By August of the following year, unemployment had soared to a half million and the seven million dollars that Chicagoans had raised for poor relief was spent—but another twenty million dollars had been raised for the World's Fair, which was to mark Chicago's "century of life and progress." The city had no credit left; it was without resources to pay the salaries of its schoolteachers, firemen, and police.

Dawes

Central to the economic mess in Chicago was the man who started the ball rolling against Capone, Charles Dawes. On June 17, 1932, Dawes walked into a meeting of the directors of the Central Republic Bank and Trust Company of Chicago and demanded that he be elected chairman of its board. The bank was in trouble as was every bank in the United States. Dawes's own holdings in the Central Republic amounted to fifty-two shares, with a market value on that day of only $2,444. The Central Republic had come out of a merger of the Central Trust Company of Illinois—which Dawes had founded but with which he had no active connection following his election to the vice presidency of the United States—with the National Bank of the Republic.[4]

Banks in the Chicago area had been taking a beating. On June 22, bank runs began in Chicago's Loop. On June 23, a chain of seven banks in the city failed to open. On June 24, eight more banks remained closed. At the end of the week, the Central Republic and four other big banks in Chicago had alone managed to stay open. But on June 25, a Saturday, long lines formed in front of the tellers' windows in the five big downtown banks. Rumors had spread through the city that even the big five were no longer solvent.

That Sunday Dawes summoned the other Chicago bankers and announced that, on Monday morning, the Central Republic Bank would not open its doors. At the behest of the other Chicago bankers and President Hoover, Dawes changed his mind and secured a loan from the Reconstruction Finance Corporation (RFC) to keep the Central Republic open. At first, Dawes hesitated to do it because he had been but recently a director of the RFC, and he did not think it would look right for him to become a borrower from it. Nevertheless, the details of the loan were arranged, and the RFC put $40,000,000 into the bank's vault. As collateral for the loan, the RFC took practically all the assets of the bank.

The decline in the value of the Central Republic's collateral required a stockholders' assessment. The RFC filed suit in 1936. Without waiting for a decision, Dawes paid his assessment of $5,200. On May 1, 1937, a federal judge ruled that the stockholders were liable to assessments but imposed the condition that executions could not be levied for six months. Yet two days after the decree, Dawes Brothers, Inc., paid $1,027,000 to the bank receiver.[5]

Despite the fact that Dawes had assumed the burden of the bank's trouble when his personal holdings were small and he had not been an officer or director of the bank for seven years, the RFC loan became the subject of attacks during the 1932 presidential campaign. Those attacks may have tarnished Dawes's national reputation, but they had no effect on how Chicagoans felt about the former vice president. Chicago considered him its most beloved citizen until 1951 when he died.[6]

Massee and Goddard

Burt Massee, the financier of the Scientific Crime Detection Laboratory, also fell victim to the Depression. Massee suffered significant losses in the stock market in 1932 and was unable to shoulder the burden of the lab by himself. The private financial backing that had been supporting the lab was withdrawn, and in April the board of directors transferred ownership of the lab to Northwestern University.

Northwestern adopted the lab as an integral part of the law school and sheared the lab's expenses to a minimum. Non-income-producers were dropped from the payroll, and the *American Journal of Police Science* was incorporated into another Northwestern-sponsored publication, the *Journal of Criminal Law and Criminology*. Northwestern terminated most of the original employees, retaining only a skeleton staff to keep the lab alive. Even Calvin Goddard, the director, had to resign because the university could no longer pay him. By 1933, the paid members of the laboratory staff had been reduced to three.

Northwestern sold the lab to the city of Chicago in 1938 for twenty-five thousand dollars. This was about one-tenth of the amount spent to develop it during its nine years and less than half the cost of its physical equipment alone.[7] Ironically, the crime lab today is operated by the very agency that its founders wanted to avoid—the Chicago Police Department. It is currently located on the fifth floor of the police headquarters annex at 1121 South State Street.

Calvin Goddard's career in firearms identification and criminalistics went into decline following the termination of his directorship, and by 1935 it had ended. His dismissal from the crime lab was not without rancor, for he tried to interest federal postal inspectors in charging his successor as director, Newman Baker, with the crime of opening his mail. During the summer of 1933, Goddard opened a sideshow at the World's Fair in Chicago. The show featured crime detection lab exhibits, crime horrors, methods of torture, an electric chair, and for a while, Dorothy Pollock, billed as "Chicago's most beautiful murderess." Later, after testifying in a murder trial in Washington, D.C., Goddard was sued for $750,000 and thereafter stated he would never handle another firearms case. He briefly reentered the field at the close of World War II to command the U.S. Army Criminal Investigation Laboratory of the Far East Command in Tokyo.[8]

McCormick

Colonel Robert McCormick, whose determination to pursue Jake Lingle's killers played a part in the downfall of Al Capone, was also hurt by the Depression. Circulation of the *Tribune* dropped and ad linage fell.[9]

In the late 1930s Colonel McCormick emerged as a leading spokesman for conservative opposition to labor and the New Deal. At the same time, the issue of fascist aggression came to the fore. McCormick's advocacy of neutralism in the isolationist-interventionist debate of World War II engendered bitterness toward him. He became such a hated figure in the United States during World War II that it was unfashionable to give him credit for anything—not even his significant contribution to the fall of Al Capone.[10] The colonel died in 1955 and was buried in his old 1918 military uniform.[11]

Chamberlin and the Crime Commission

The Depression forced Chamberlin to shift the Crime Commission's focus from public enemies to fund raising. Delivering a report on the financial status of the Commission to its board of directors on November 19, 1931, Chamberlin said:

> As you gentlemen know the situation has been tense because of the Depression. George Paddock, the chairman of the finance committee, and I have done everything but sit on the steps of the library with a tin cup and lead pencils. . . . The staff of the Operating Department has been reduced from forty-two to twenty-five. The working hours of the remaining employees has been increased eight hours a week. . . . The salaries of the employees still on the payroll will be cut five and ten per cent where the weekly pay is more than $25. In addition to this, the salaries of the Operating Director and the Assistant Operating Director will be entirely suspended and held in abeyance pending a readjustment.[12]

Chamberlin remained with the Crime Commission through the hard times. Following the Depression, Chamberlin drafted two legislative bills, one concerning carrying concealed weapons and the other, vagrancy, that were enacted into law. As a result of his own study of the parole system in Illinois in 1934, Chamberlin developed an appreciation of the positive functions of parole. His views toward delinquents and criminals turned progressive in the late 1930s as was evidenced by his support for Illinois' indeterminate sentence law in 1937 and his endorsement of the Chicago Area Project in 1938. When Chamberlin died in 1941, a Commission press release stated that "he was respected even by those whom, during his lifetime, he opposed."[13]

The Secret Six

Although the Crime Commission survived the Depression, the Secret Six did not. Samuel Insull, the main financial backer of the Secret Six, watched as his utilities empire collapsed in 1932 with a loss to investors of $785 million.[14] The failure of Insull's gas and electric business that had operated in over thirty states caused Insull to flee to Paris.

The battle to extradite him from Greece shared the front pages with the New Deal, Adolf Hitler, and the Lindbergh baby. Insull's trials for mail fraud, embezzlement, and violation of the federal bankruptcy acts resulted in acquittals. Nevertheless, the criminal charges, coupled with the fact that his was "the biggest business failure in the history of the world," ruined Insull's reputation. He died in 1938 owing $14,000,000.[15]

The departure of Samuel Insull plus the deaths of two other members of the Secret Six, Julius Rosenwald in 1932 and Edward E. Gore in 1935, dealt a severe blow to the vigilante outfit. Other businessmen, faced with the necessity of cutting both their personal budgets and the expenses of the companies they led, became reluctant to contribute to the Secret Six because of a scandal that broke in 1932.

"SWANSON SLEUTH CAUGHT TAPPING TELEPHONE WIRE OF 'SECRET SIX' OFFICE" blurted out a headline in the *Chicago Daily News* on August 31, 1932. Seizure of a state's attorney's operative tapping the telephone wires of the Secret Six revealed that Alexander G. Jamie, director of operations for the Secret Six, had been investigating the state's attorney's office. Jamie's detectives seized the wiretapper in the act of tapping a secret Loop office maintained by the Secret Six. Photographs taken by Jamie's agents of the operative in the act of tapping the wires were published in all the major Chicago newspapers. Accusations flew back and forth between the Secret Six and State's Attorney Swanson. The Secret Six charged Swanson with selling minutes of grand jury proceedings to defense attorneys; State's Attorney Swanson claimed the Secret Six had come under the domination of one of the Secret Six's own detectives, an unsavory character named Shirley Kub.

Looking into this bizarre situation, a grand jury grilled Robert Isham Randolph, the leader of the Secret Six. Randolph took the Fifth Amendment several times during his testimony. The jury cleared Swanson of any wrongdoing but dug up some dirt on the Secret Six. It discovered that Kub was a thief, a con artist, and a bigamist; that bankers and other wealthy businessmen were paying Randolph $12,000 a year to head the Secret Six, while at the same time Randolph was receiving $12,000 a year as an engineer on the sanitary district payroll.[16]

The final setback for the Secret Six came in December 1932 when a jury awarded $30,000 to William S. Kuhn, Jr. Kuhn had sought damages on charges of false arrest and malicious persecution because of his arrest in 1930 by the Secret Six on the charge of sending extortion letters to Marion Wright, debutante daughter of William Van Doren Wright, steel company executive. Criminal charges against Kuhn were dismissed, but a jury held Alexander Jamie and Edgar Dudley, one of Jamie's assistants, liable for the damages incurred by Kuhn.[17]

On April 19, 1933, the Chicago Association of Commerce disbanded the Secret Six.[18]

Robert Isham Randolph emerged from the scandals with his reputation still intact. He moved on to become the director of operations at Chicago's World's Fair. He did, however, encounter the Capone gang once more. On the night of June 8, 1934, Joseph ("Violets") Fusco, Matthew ("Mimi") Capone, Dennis ("Duke") Cooney, and Ralph ("Bottles") Capone went to the opening of the Old Mexico exhibit to see Rosalia, the fan dancer. Just before Rosalia made her appearance, Randolph and twenty-five fair police officers escorted Fusco, Cooney, and the two Capone brothers to jail. The hoodlums were not doing anything but munching on sandwiches and drinking beer when Randolph had them arrested, but as the colonel explained to newspaper reporters, "The reputation of the fair must be maintained."[19]

Shortly thereafter Randolph gained the Republican nomination for state representative of the Sixth District in Illinois but lost the election to a Democrat. When World War II broke out, Randolph, a World War I veteran, reenlisted in the U.S. Army. The leader of the once-famous Secret Six was released in 1943 because, at age 60, the Army considered him too old.[20] He died eight years later.

George A. Paddock, another member of the Secret Six, went on to enjoy a successful political career. The first time a political party used systematic direct mail was in 1936 when Paddock raised money for the GOP National Committee. In 1940 Paddock was elected U.S. congressman of the Tenth Illinois District. His most noteworthy deeds included an effort to publicize the wretched living conditions in the slums of Washington, D.C., and an attempt to secure legislation mandating adequate standards regarding light, sanitation, and floor space in federal housing. Congressman Paddock's work on behalf of the cause of decent housing can scarcely be overemphasized because it came at a time when the vast influx of war workers intensified congestion in the nation's slums. Loyalty to his country led Paddock to attempt to reenlist in the military during World War II, but the Army said it could not use him. So Paddock returned to Chicago where he became a stockbroker again. Paddock drove himself hard—the stock market wasn't lucrative then—and that, plus the political disappointments and arteriosclerosis, finally brought on a nervous breakdown in the 1950s and death in 1964.[21]

The final member of the Secret Six, Frank J. Loesch, devoted his later years to advocating changes to strengthen the criminal justice system. He proposed consolidation of the city and county police into a single statewide force as a means of eliminating duplication of effort and bringing more efficiency to law enforcement.[22] To minimize the intrusion of politics into the administration of justice, he urged lawmakers to modify statutes so that prosecutors and judges would be appointed instead of elected.[23] He wanted to alter the Eighteenth Amendment so citizens could purchase "a reasonable amount of alcohol for personal use."[24] Before Loesch died at age ninety-two, the Rotary Club bestowed upon him the award of "Chicago's Most Valuable citizen."[25]

Did the Crime Crusaders Make a Difference?

History shows that Capone's ultimate arrest, prosecution, conviction, and imprisonment were the result of a private-public partnership. But for the efforts of the crime crusaders, Capone's long immunity from the law would not have been broken, his image would not have changed from public benefactor to public enemy, and Chicago's reputation would not have been redeemed in time for the 1933 World's Fair.

Yet, the crime crusaders couldn't pat themselves on the back. Despite the incapacitation of Al Capone and other public enemies, the syndicate persisted. Prohibition made a Capone inevitable, and by the time the Eighteenth Amendment was repealed in 1933, Frank Nitti and Capone's other powerful successors had diversified the syndicate's portfolio of illicit holdings so that the mob was no longer dependent upon bootlegging. Hence, it must be conceded that the crime crusaders ultimately failed to eliminate the syndicate from Chicago.

Nevertheless, the crime crusaders made a lasting contribution. They showed that businessmen could stand up for themselves and their city in the face of political disorganization and personal danger. If there is a lesson to be learned from the crime crusaders, it is revealed in the following excerpt from an obituary written for Frank Loesch in 1944: "He demonstrated two things: first, that decency CAN prevail, with courageous leadership, over even the most powerful alliance of crime and crookedness; and second, that a man's years are no fit gauge of his capacity for usefulness."[26]

Notes

Index

Notes

1. The Rest of the Al Capone Story

1. Robert Isham Randolph Scrapbooks, IV (1921–1946), Chicago Historical Society.
2. Randolph Scrapbooks, IV.
3. Eliot Ness and Oscar Fraley, *The Untouchables* (New York: Pocket Books, 1987), p. 6.
4. Ness and Fraley, p. 11.
5. Ness and Fraley, p. 45.
6. Elmer L. Irey, *The Tax Dodgers: The Inside Story of the T-Men's War with America's Political and Underworld Hoodlums* (New York: Greenberg, 1948).
7. John Kobler, *Capone: The Life and World of Al Capone* (New York: G. P. Putnam's Sons, 1971).
8. Robert J. Schoenberg, *Mr. Capone: The Real—and Complete—Story of Al Capone* (New York: William Morrow and Company, Inc., 1992).
9. George Murray, *The Legacy of Al Capone* (New York: G. P. Putnam's Sons, 1975), p. 134.
10. *Chicago Tribune* (October 18, 1931).
11. Timothy Samuelson, "Nomination of Alphonse Capone's Residence for Inclusion on the National Register of Historic Places," U.S. Department of the Interior, National Park Service (1988), p. 1.
12. *Chicago Tribune* (August 1, 1930).
13. Irv Letofsky, "Harmless as a Puppydog," book review in the *Los Angeles Times* (August 23, 1992), p. 12.
14. Samuelson, p. 8.
15. *Chicago Tribune* (January 16, 1920).
16. *Chicago Tribune* (January 16, 1920).

2. Who Were the Crime Crusaders?

1. Fred D. Pasley, *Al Capone: The Biography of a Self-Made Man* (Binghamton, New York: Ives Washburn Publisher, 1930), p. 149.
2. Bascom N. Timmons, *Portrait of an American: Charles G. Dawes* (New York: Henry Holt and Company, 1953), pp. 3–16.
3. Glenn A. Bishop and Paul T. Gilbert, *Chicago's Accomplishments and Leaders* (Chicago: Bishop Publishing Company, 1932), p. 147.
4. Timmons, pp. 211–212.

5. Timmons, p. 229.

6. Timmons, p. 161.

7. Bishop and Gilbert, p. 307; Lloyd Lewis and Henry Justin Smith, *Chicago: The History of Its Reputation* (New York: Harcourt, Brace and Company, 1929), pp. 482–483.

8. Lewis and Smith, pp. 482–483.

9. Letter from Benjamin Wham to Henry Barrett Chamberlin (August 15, 1944), Chicago Crime Commission files.

10. Frank J. Loesch, "Crime as a Breakdown of Citizenship," in American Institute of Sacred Literature, ed., *Building a Moral Reserve or the Civic Responsibilities of a Christian Citizen* (Chicago: University of Chicago Press, 1930), pp. 63–77.

11. Frank J. Loesch, *Personal Experiences During the Chicago Fire. 1871* (Chicago: Personally printed, 1925), p. 8.

12. *Chicago Daily News* (April 24, 1929).

13. *Chicago Tribune* (May 23, 1972).

14. *Chicago Daily News* (April 16, 1929).

15. Joseph Duayne Dillon, "A History of Criminalistics in the United States, 1850–1950" (Ph.D. dissertation, University of California at Berkeley, 1977), pp. 118–120.

16. Dillon, p. 143.

17. Joseph Gies, *The Colonel of Chicago* (New York: Dutton, 1979), pp. 1–2.

18. Gies, p. 9.

19. Bishop and Gilbert, p. 327.

20. James Doherty, "History of the Chicago Crime Commission," *Police Digest* (December 1960), p. 15.

21. Doherty, p. 15.

22. *Bulletin of the Chicago Crime Commission* (September 12, 1921), p. 2.

23. *Bulletin of the Chicago Crime Commission* (September 12, 1921), p. 2.

24. *Bulletin of the Chicago Crime Commission* (September 12, 1921), p. 2.

25. Bishop and Gilbert, p. 383.

3. Why the Feds Stepped In

1. John Kobler, *Capone: The Life and World of Al Capone* (New York: G. P. Putnam's Sons, 1971), pp. 229–230.

2. *Literary Digest* (March 20, 1926), p. 7.

3. *Chicago Tribune* (February 28, 1926).

4. *Chicago Tribune* (February 28, 1926).

5. Kobler, p. 167.

6. *Chicago Tribune* (March 3, 1926).

7. *Literary Digest* (March 20, 1926), p. 7.

8. *Chicago Tribune* (March 6, 1926).

9. *Literary Digest* (March 20, 1926).

10. *Chicago Tribune* (May 1, 1926).

11. *Chicago Tribune* (May 5, 1926).

12. John Landesco, *Organized Crime in Chicago*, Part III of the Illinois Crime Survey (Chicago: University of Chicago Press, 1929), p. 16.

13. Landesco, p. 17.

14. Landesco, p. 23.

15. Herbert Ashbury, *Gem of the Prairie: An Informal History of the Chicago Underworld* (New York: Garden City Publishers, 1942), p. 102; Landesco, p. 132.

16. *Chicago Tribune* (October 22, 1926); George Murray, *The Legacy of Al Capone* (New York: G. P. Putnam's Sons, 1975), pp. 129–132.

17. Murray, p. 149.

18. Murray, pp. 149–150.

19. Murray, p. 151.

20. Charles G. Dawes, *Notes as Vice-President. 1928–1929* (Boston: Little, Brown, and Company, 1935), pp. 77–78.

21. *Chicago Tribune* (October 10, 1931).

4. Frank J. Loesch and the Quest for Free Elections

1. *Chicago Daily News* (April 3, 1928).

2. Fred D. Pasley, *Al Capone: The Biography of a Self-Made Man* (Binghamton, New York: Ives Washburn Publisher, 1930), p. 201.

3. *Chicago Daily News* (April 11, 1928).

4. Pasley, pp. 217–218.

5. *Chicago Herald and Examiner* (April 12, 1928).

6. John Landesco, *Organized Crime in Chicago* (Chicago: University of Chicago Press, 1929), p. 13.

7. *Chicago Daily News* (May 26, 1928).

8. *Chicago Daily News* (June 1, 1928).

9. *Chicago Daily News* (June 4, 1928).

10. *Chicago Daily News* (June 4, 1928).

11. *Chicago Daily News* (June 18, 1928).

12. *Chicago Daily News* (June 19, 1928).

13. *Chicago Daily News* (June 26, 1928).

14. *Chicago Daily News* (June 30 and July 3, 1928).

15. *Chicago Daily News* (July 10, 1928).

16. *Chicago Daily News* (July 10, 1928).

17. *Chicago Daily News* (July 15, 1928).

18. *Chicago Daily News* (July 19, 1928).

19. *Chicago Daily News* (July 20, 1928).

20. *Chicago Daily News* (July 21, 1928).

21. *Chicago Daily News* (July 21 and 25, 1928).
22. *Chicago Daily News* (July 23, 1928).
23. *Chicago Daily News* (July 31, 1928).
24. *Chicago Daily News* (July 31, 1928).
25. *Chicago Daily News* (July 31, 1928).
26. *Chicago Daily News* (July 31, 1928).
27. *Chicago Daily News* (August 4, 1928).
28. *Chicago Daily News* (September 18, 1928).
29. *Chicago Daily News* (September 18, 1928).
30. *Chicago Daily News* (September 20, 1928).
31. *Chicago Daily News* (October 13, 1928).
32. *Chicago Daily News* (October 14, 1928).
33. *Chicago Daily News* (August 22, 1928).
34. *Chicago Daily News* (October 16, 1928).
35. *Chicago Daily News* (October 16, 1928).
36. *Chicago Daily News* (October 17, 1928).
37. *Chicago Daily News* (October 3, 1928).
38. *Chicago Daily News* (November 3, 1928).
39. *Chicago Tribune* (March 25, 1931).
40. John Kobler, *Capone: The Life and World of Al Capone* (New York: G. P. Putnam's Sons, 1971), p. 16.
41. *Chicago Daily News* (November 7, 1928).
42. *Chicago Daily News* (November 7, 1928).
43. *Chicago Daily News* (November 23, 1928).
44. *Chicago Daily News* (November 23, 1928).
45. *Chicago Daily News* (November 23, 1928).
46. *Chicago Daily News* (November 23, 1928).
47. *Chicago Daily News* (November 24, 1928).
48. *Chicago Daily News* (November 27, 1928).
49. *Chicago Daily News* (March 19, 1929).
50. Herbert Hoover, *Public Papers of the Presidents of the United States. Herbert Hoover: Concerning the Public Messages, Speeches and Statements of the President, January 1 to December 31, 1930* (Washington, D.C.: U.S. Government Printing Office, 1976), pp. 276–277.
51. John H. Lyle, *The Dry and Lawless Years* (Englewood Cliffs, New Jersey: Prentice-Hall, Inc., 1961), p. 249.
52. *Chicago Daily News* (April 21, 1929).
53. *Chicago Daily News* (March 12 and 18, 1929).
54. *Chicago Daily News* (May 21, 1929).
55. *Chicago Daily News* (June 17, 1929).
56. *Chicago Daily News* (June 12, 1929).
57. *Chicago Daily News* (June 12, 1929).
58. *Chicago Daily News* (June 13, 1929).
59. *Chicago Daily News* (June 12, 1929).
60. *Chicago Daily News* (October 4, 1929).

61. *Chicago Daily News* (October 12 and 20, 1929).

62. *Chicago Daily News* (November 20 and 21, 1929).

63. *Chicago Daily News* (November 22, 1929).

64. *Chicago Daily News* (November 22 and 23, 1929).

65. *Chicago Daily News* (November 27, 1929).

66. Louther S. Horne, "Loesch Tells How to Beat Crime," *New York Times Magazine* (April 10, 1938), p. 8.

67. *Chicago Daily News* (November 20, 1929).

68. *Chicago Daily News* (April 26, 1929).

5. Chicago's Answer to the St. Valentine's Day Massacre

1. Calvin Goddard, "The Valentine Day Massacre: A Study in Ammunition Tracing." *American Journal of Police Science I* (January–February 1930), pp. 60–78.

2. Kenneth Allsop, *The Bootleggers and Their Era* (Garden City, New York: Double day and Company, Inc., 1961), p. 139.

3. *Chicago Tribune* (February 15, 1929).

4. Allsop, p. 142.

5. Fred Inbau, "Science Versus the Criminal," *Northwestern University Alumni News* (n.d.): 7–10.

6. *Chicago Daily News* (February 15, 1929).

7. *Chicago Daily News* (February 15, 1929).

8. *Chicago Daily News* (February 16, 1929).

9. *Chicago Daily News* (February 16, 1929).

10. *Chicago Daily News* (February 18, 1929).

11. *Chicago Daily News* (February 16, 1929).

12. *Chicago Daily News* (February 16, 1929).

13. John Kobler, *Capone: the Life and World of Al Capone* (New York: G. P. Putnam's Sons, 1971) p. 248.

14. Fred Pasley, *Al Capone: The Biography of a Self-Made Man* (Binghamton, New York: Ives Washburn Publisher, 1930), pp. 259–260.

15. *Chicago Daily News* (February 22, 1929).

16. *Chicago Daily News* (February 27, 1929).

17. *Chicago Daily News* (March 1, 1929).

18. *Chicago Daily News* (December 2, 1929).

19. Kobler, p. 256.

20. *Chicago Daily News* (March 8, 1929).

21. *Chicago Daily News* (March 20, 1929).

22. Kobler, pp. 258–260.

23. *Chicago Tribune* (May 18, 1929).

24. Goddard, p. 62.

25. *Chicago Daily News* (April 13, 1929).

26. *Chicago Daily News* (April 15, 1929).

27. *Chicago Tribune* (April 14, 1929).

28. *Chicago Daily News* (April 2, 1929).

29. *Chicago Post* (February 23, 1929).

30. Kobler, p. 253.

31. *Chicago Daily News* (April 19, 1929).

32. Letter from John Henry Wigmore to Albert J. Harno, dean of the University of Illinois (April 19, 1938), John Henry Wigmore Papers, Northwestern University Archives Series 17/9.

33. John Henry Wigmore, "The Massee Crime Detection Laboratory Project" (June 1, 1929), John Henry Wigmore Papers, Northwestern University Archives Series 17/9.

34. Calvin Goddard, "Purpose of the Journal," *American Journal of Police Science* I (January–February 1930), pp. 1–7.

35. Calvin Goddard, "Scientific Crime Detection Laboratories in Europe," *American Journal of Police Science* I (January–February 1930), p. 13.

36. *Chicago Daily News* (July 14, 1929).

37. Letter from John Henry Wigmore to Lawrence B. Dunham, director of the Bureau of Social Hygiene, New York (December 27, 1929), John Henry Wigmore Papers, Northwestern University Archives Series 17/9.

38. *Chicago Daily News* (December 17, 1929).

39. *Chicago Daily News* (January 18, 1930).

40. *Chicago Daily News* (January 18, 1930).

41. *Chicago Daily News* (January 18, 1930).

42. *Chicago Daily News* (December 24, 1929).

43. Goddard, "The Valentine Day Massacre," p. 78.

44. *Chicago Tribune* (April 28, 1931).

45. John Henry Wigmore, "Scientific Crime Detection Laboratory: Its Origins and Development with Proposals for Expansion," unpublished paper (1932), John Henry Wigmore Papers, Northwestern University Archives 17/9.

46. Joseph Duayne Dillon, *A History of Criminalistics in the United States, 1850–1950.* (Ph.D. dissertation, University of California at Berkeley, 1977), pp. 8–9.

47. "Scientific Crime Detection Laboratory," *Northwestern University Bulletin* XXXII (February 8, 1932).

48. Dennis E. Hoffman, "Yesterday's City: Crime-Fighting Scientists," *Chicago History* (Spring and Summer, 1990), pp. 95–96.

49. Eloise Keeler, *Lie Detector Man.* (New York: Telshare Publishing, Inc., 1984).

6. The Colonel, Jake, and Scarface Al

1. John Boettiger, *Jake Lingle or Chicago on the Spot* (New York: E. P. Dutton and Co., Inc., 1931), p. 18; *Chicago Tribune* (June 10, 1930).

2. Boettiger, p. 19; *Chicago Tribune* (July 31, 1930).

3. Robert Rutherford McCormick, "The Lingle Case," an address broadcast over WGN, WGNB, and the Mutual Broadcasting System (October 16, 1954).

4. *Chicago Tribune* (June 10, 1930).

5. *Chicago Tribune* (June 10, 1930).

6. *Chicago Tribune* (June 10, 1930).

7. *Chicago Tribune* (June 11, 1930).

8. *Chicago Tribune* (June 11, 1930).

9. *Chicago Tribune* (June 10 and 30, 1931); Boettiger, pp. 25–40.

10. *Chicago Tribune* (June 10, 1930).

11. *Chicago Tribune* (June 30, 1930).

12. *Chicago Tribune* (June 21, 1930).

13. Boettiger, p. 37.

14. Boettiger, pp. 35–39.

15. *Chicago Tribune* (June 13, 1930).

16. *Chicago Tribune* (April 8, 1931).

17. Boettiger, pp. 58–59.

18. *Chicago Tribune* (June 18, 1930).

19. *Chicago Tribune* (June 29, 1930).

20. *Chicago Tribune* (June 29, 1930).

21. *Chicago Tribune* (June 29, 1930).

22. *Chicago Tribune* (June 29, 1930).

23. *Chicago Daily News* (July 5, 1930); Boettiger, pp. 46–49.

24. Boettiger, pp. 74–79.

25. *Chicago Tribune* (June 12, 1930).

26. *Chicago Herald and Examiner* (June 21, 1930).

27. *Los Angeles Examiner* (June 22, 1930).

28. *Chicago Herald and Examiner* (June 22, 1930).

29. *Chicago Tribune* (July 2, 1930).

30. *Chicago Tribune* (July 3, 1930).

31. Boettiger, p. 85.

32. *Chicago Tribune* (July 16, 1930).

33. *Chicago Daily News* (July 9, 1930).

34. *Chicago Daily News* (July 11, 1930).

35. *Chicago Tribune* (July 12, 1930).

36. *Chicago Tribune* (July 20, 1930).

37. *Chicago Tribune* (August 1, 1930).

38. Boettiger, p. 168.

39. Boettiger, p. 169.

40. Boettiger, pp. 170–176.

41. Boettiger, pp. 178–188.

42. Boettiger, p. 189.

43. Boettiger, pp. 189–191.

44. Boettiger, pp. 227–232.

45. Boettiger, pp. 234–245.
46. Boettiger, pp. 251–273.
47. Boettiger, pp. 275–276.
48. Boettiger, pp. 287–300.
49. Boettiger, pp. 302–314.
50. *Chicago Tribune* (June 9, 1931).

7. Labeling Capone

1. Fred D. Pasley, *Al Capone: The Biography of a Self-Made Man* (Binghamton, New York: Ives Washburn, 1930), p. 351.
2. *Chicago Tribune* (April 24, 1930).
3. *Chicago Tribune* (April 24, 1930).
4. *Chicago Tribune* (April 24, 1930).
5. James Doherty, "History of the Chicago Crime Commission," *Police Digest* (December 1960), p. 18.
6. Memo from Henry Barrett Chamberlin to Frank J. Loesch (July 8, 1930), Chicago Crime Commission files.
7. Radio talk given by Henry Barrett Chamberlin on station WBBM in Chicago (February 11, 1931), Chicago Crime Commission files.
8. Chicago Crime Commission, *Criminal Justice* (May 1930).
9. *Chicago Daily News* (June 23, 1930).
10. *Chicago American* (June 28, 1930).
11. *Chicago Herald and Examiner* (April 24, 1930).
12. *Chicago Tribune* (April 26, 1930), p. 1.
13. *Chicago Tribune* (May 10, 1930).
14. *Chicago Tribune* (May 21, 1930).
15. *Chicago Tribune* (May 21, 1930).
16. *Chicago Tribune* (September 10, 1930).
17. John H. Lyle, *The Dry and Lawless Years* (Englewood Cliffs, New Jersey: Prentice-Hall, Inc., 1961), p. 233.
18. Lyle, pp. 233–234.
19. Lyle, pp. 234.
20. *Chicago Tribune* (September 17, 1930).
21. *Chicago Tribune* (September 17, 1930).
22. *Chicago Tribune* (September 18, 1930).
23. *Chicago Tribune* (September 19, 1930).
24. *Chicago Tribune* (September 24, 1930).
25. *Chicago Tribune* (September 24, 1930).
26. *Chicago Tribune* (September 26, 1930).
27. *Chicago Tribune* (September 27, 1930).
28. *Chicago Tribune* (September 27, 1930).
29. *Chicago Tribune* (September 27, 1930).
30. John Boettiger, *Jake Lingle or Chicago on the Spot* (New York: E. P. Dutton and Co., Inc., 1931), pp. 142–143.

31. *Chicago Tribune* (September 26, 1930).

32. *Chicago Tribune* (October 3, 1930).

33. *Chicago Tribune* (October 3, 1930).

34. *Chicago Tribune* (October 10, 1930).

35. *Chicago Tribune* (October 10, 1930).

36. *Chicago Tribune* (February 6, 1931).

37. *Chicago Tribune* (October 10, 1930).

38. *Chicago Tribune* (February 18, 1931).

39. *Chicago Tribune* (October 5, 1930).

40. *Chicago Tribune* (October 7, 1930).

41. *People ex rel James "Fur" Sammons v. Snow*, 340 Ill. 464.

42. *Chicago Tribune* (October 17, 1930).

43. *People v. Belcastro*, 356 Ill. 144.

44. Lyle, p. 131.

45. *Chicago Tribune* (October 24, 1930).

46. *Chicago Tribune* (October 24, 1930).

47. *Chicago Tribune* (November 4, 1930).

48. *Chicago Tribune* (November 11, 1930).

49. *Chicago Tribune* (November 14, 1930).

50. *Chicago Tribune* (November 14, 1930).

51. Kenneth Allsop, *The Bootleggers and Their Era* (Garden City, New York: Doubleday and Company, Inc., 1961), p. 324.

52. *Chicago Tribune* (December 1, 1930).

53. *Chicago Tribune* (December 8, 1930).

54. *Chicago Tribune* (December 13, 1930).

55. *Chicago Tribune* (December 16, 1930).

56. *Chicago Tribune* (December 19, 1930).

57. *Chicago Tribune* (December 27, 1930).

58. *Chicago Tribune* (February 7, 1930).

59. *Chicago Tribune* (February 14, 1931).

60. *Chicago Tribune* (February 17, 1931).

61. *Chicago Tribune* (February 23, 1931).

62. *Chicago Tribune* (February 25, 1931).

63. *Chicago Tribune* (February 28, 1931).

64. *Chicago Times* (March 4, 1931).

65. *Chicago Daily News* (March 20, 1931).

66. Report on Alphonse Capone's Vagrancy Case (1931), Chicago Crime Commission files.

67. *Chicago Daily News* (April 3, 1931).

68. Allsop, p. 329.

69. *Chicago Herald and Examiner* (June 5, 1931).

70. *Chicago Post* (June 4, 1931).

71. *Chicago Post* (June 4, 1931).

72. *Chicago Tribune* (August 1, 1931).

73. *Chicago Herald and Examiner* (August 3, 1931).

74. *Chicago Herald and Examiner* (August 3, 1931).
75. *Chicago Herald and Examiner* (August 3, 1931).
76. *Chicago Herald and Examiner* (August 3, 1931).

8. The Mystery of the Secret Six

1. *Washington Post* (August 21, 1932).
2. *Washington Post* (August 21, 1932).
3. *Chicago Daily News* (February 20, 1930).
4. Robert Isham Randolph, "Business Fights Crime in Chicago," *Saturday Evening Post* (August 16, 1930), p. 13.
5. Robert Isham Randolph Scrapbooks, III (1921–1946). Chicago Historical Society.
6. Randolph Scrapbooks, I.
7. Randolph Scrapbooks, I.
8. *Chicago Post* (February 8, 1930).
9. *Chicago Daily News* (February 17, 1930).
10. *Chicago Tribune* (April 4, 1930).
11. *Toronto Star* (April 10, 1930).
12. *Chicago Tribune* (October 31, 1931).
13. Telephone interview with Mrs. Wallace Jamie, the daughter-in-law of Alexander Jamie, on July 16, 1990.
14. *Chicago Tribune* (May 9, 1930).
15. Robert Isham Randolph, "How to Wreck Capone's Gang," *Collier's* (March 7, 1931), p. 8.
16. Randolph, p. 9.
17. Randolph, p. 9.
18. Eliot Ness and Oscar Fraley, *The Untouchables* (New York: Pocket Books, 1987), p. 7.
19. John Kobler, *Capone: The Life and World of Al Capone* (New York: G. P. Putnam's Sons, 1971), p. 266.
20. Randolph Scrapbooks, IV.
21. James Dubro and Robin F. Rowland, *King of the Mob* (New York: Penguin, 1987), p. 233.
22. Randolph Scrapbooks, IV.
23. *Chicago Tribune* (July 29, 1930).
24. *Chicago Daily News* (November 12, 1930).
25. *Chicago Evening Post* (March 3, 1931).
26. Randolph Scrapbooks, III.
27. Kenneth Allsop, *The Bootleggers and Their Era* (Garden City, New York: Doubleday and Company, 1961), pp. 225–226.
28. *Chicago Tribune* (April 8, 1931).
29. Elmer L. Irey, *The Tax Dodgers: The Inside Story of the T-Men's War with America's Political and Underworld Hoodlums* (New York: Greenberg, 1948), p. 36.

30. Irey, p. 40.
31. Irey, p. 45.
32. Irey, p. 47.
33. Kobler, p. 275.
34. *Chicago Tribune* (November 13, 1930).
35. *Chicago Tribune* (November 13, 1930).
36. Randolph Scrapbooks, III.
37. Randolph Scrapbooks, III.
38. Randolph Scrapbooks, III.
39. *Chicago Tribune* (December 21, 1930).
40. Randolph Scrapbooks, III.
41. Kobler, p. 318.
42. Irey, p. 52.
43. Irey, p. 53.
44. Kobler, p. 319.
45. Randolph Scrapbooks, III.
46. Kobler, p. 322.
47. Robert Ross, *The Trial of Al Capone* (Chicago: Robert Ross, Publisher, 1933), p. 47.
48. Ross, pp. 49–50.
49. *Chicago Tribune* (October 9, 1931).
50. *Chicago Tribune* (October 14, 1931).
51. Transcripts of *U.S. v. Capone* (1931), pp. 1–27 of the Ries Testimony.
52. *Chicago Tribune* (October 15, 1931).
53. *Chicago Tribune* (October 18, 1931).
54. *Chicago Tribune* (October 18, 1931).
55. *Chicago Tribune* (October 25, 1931).
56. Randolph Scrapbooks, III.
57. Randolph Scrapbooks, V.
58. U.S. Bureau of Investigation, Reports on the Secret Six (1931), Federal Bureau of Investigation, Washington, D.C.
59. *Chicago Daily News* (January 20, 1932); *Chicago Tribune* (March 16, 1943).
60. John H. Lyle, *The Dry and Lawless Years* (Englewood Cliffs, New Jersey: Prentice-Hall, Inc., 1961), pp. 197 and 234.
61. Chicago Crime Commission, Minutes of Executive Committee Meetings (March 10, 1931), Chicago Crime Commission files.
62. *Chicago Tribune* (October 18, 1931).

9. Whatever Happened to the Crime Crusaders?

1. Chicago American (October 26, 1931).
2. *Chicago Daily News* (October 27, 1931).

3. Kenneth Allsop, *The Bootleggers and Their Era* (Garden City, New York: Doubleday and Company, Inc., 1961), pp. 252–253.

4. Bascom N. Timmons, *Portrait of an American: Charles G. Dawes* (New York: Henry Holt and Company, 1953), p. 316.

5. Timmons, pp. 317–337.

6. Timmons, p. 326.

7. Dennis E. Hoffman, "Yesterday's City: Crime-Fighting Scientists," *Chicago History* (Spring and Summer 1990), pp. 93–95.

8. Joseph Duayne Dillon, "A History of Criminalistics in the United States, 1850–1950" (Ph.D. dissertation, University of California at Berkeley, 1977), pp. 165–166.

9. Joseph Gies, *The Colonel of Chicago* (New York: E. P. Dutton, 1979), p. 117.

10. Letter from Joseph Gies to the author (February 4, 1990).

11. Gies, p. 235.

12. Minutes of the Board of Directors of the Chicago Crime Commission (November 19, 1931), p. 2.

13. Chicago Crime Commission, "In Memoriam of Henry Barrett Chamberlin" (1941), Chicago Crime Commission files.

14. Forrest McDonald, *Insull* (Chicago: University of Chicago Press, 1962), p. vii.

15. Allsop, p. 254.

16. U.S. Department of Justice, Bureau of Investigation, "John A. Swanson," File 62–27764.

17. *Chicago Daily News* (December 5, 1932).

18. *Chicago Daily News* (April 20, 1933).

19. *Chicago Herald and Examiner* (June 8, 1934).

20. Randolph Scrapbooks, V (1921–1946), Chicago Historical Society.

21. Letter from George Paddock, Jr., to the author (August 2, 1989).

22. *Chicago Examiner* (January 18, 1932).

23. *Chicago Daily News* (March 8, 1932).

24. *Yale News* (January 27, 1932).

25. *Chicago Daily News* (April 11, 1939).

26. *Chicago American* (August 2, 1944).

Index

Accardo, Tony, 124, 140
Ahern, Michael, 43
Aiello, Joe, 87, 111, 129
Armando, John, 37–38; 56

Barker, George "Red," 111, 133
Belcastro, James, 57, 111, 128–29
Boss, Eller's henchmen, 43–44, 49
Brooks, C. Wayland, 108
Brothers, Leo, 107–9
Brundidge, Harry T.: grand jury's assessment of his testimony, 105; his midnight visit with Capone, 102–5; stories on Lingle case, 99–100
Bundesen, Herman N., 49, 72–74, 76, 80–81, 153–54
Burke, Fred "Killer," 82, 85; indictment for murder, 87–88; police search of his house, 85. *See also* St. Valentine's Day Massacre

Cainski, Joe, 140
Campagna, Louis, 124
Campagnia, Sam, 139
Capone, Al, 4, 7; arrival at federal building in Chicago, 78; and "Big Bill" Thompson, 134, 152–53; citation for contempt of court, 79; crediting Secret Six, 164; federal indictments of; 159–60; infiltrating organized labor and city government, 110–11; meeting with Judge McGoorty, 130; meeting with Operative Number One, 106–7; motive for killing Lingle, 107; murder of Joe Aiello, 129; murders of Scalise and Anselmi, 77; at national meeting of crime bosses in Atlantic City, 79; in New York, 131; origins of nickname "Scarface Al," 5; as peacemaker, 30; plea bargaining before his tax evasion trial, 160; his plot to kill government agents, 160; in police scandal, 123; possible involvement in federal election fraud, 130; as "public enemy number one," 111; puppydog or supervillain, 7–8; refusal to answer summons, 78; rise

of, 5–7; sentence for carrying a concealed weapon in Philadelphia, 79–80; soup kitchen, 131; tax evasion trial of, 160–63; as a threat to business, 30; threats against the makers of grape concentrates, 130–31; vagrancy trial of, 135–36
Capone, Ralph, 112, 115–16, 126, 148
Cappizzio, Tony, 125
Cermak, Anton, 155
Chamberlin, Henry B., 18–20, 117; during the Depression, 169; first public enemies list, 111; and Judge Lyle, 119–20, 127, 129, 132; reaction to Winslow Brothers robbery, 18; second list of public enemies, 138; his talks on WBBM, 114
Chicago American, 165
Chicago Association of Commerce, 19, 74–75, 141, 171
Chicago Bar Association, 35, 126
Chicago Crime Commission, 13, 83, 113–15, 127–28, 136, 144, 169
Chicago Daily News, 101, 165
Chicago Herald and Examiner, 99, 138–40
Chicago police: in scandal, 122–25
Chicago Tribune, 72, 95, 100, 109, 113
Chicago World's Fair (1933), 9, 13, 31, 49, 166, 168, 171
Colosimo, James, 5
Comerford, Frank, 40
Committee on Immigration (U.S. Senate), 26–27
Coolidge, Calvin, 12, 24
Crime crusaders: activities of, 11; characteristics of, 10; vigilantes or good citizens, 21–23
Crowe, Robert E., 25–26, 28–30, 36

Dawes, Charles G.: 11–13; as ambassador to Great Britain, 33; criticism of state's attorney and sheriff, 25–26; decision *not* to coordinate forces opposed to Capone, 32; during the Depression, 166–67; petition to U.S. Senate, 24–26; putting honest U.S. attorneys in Chicago, 31–32

Index

Index

Dennis E. Hoffman is a associate professor of criminal justice at the University of Nebraska at Omaha, where he teaches courses in administration of justice and criminology. During the past five years, he has published articles and monographs about organized crime in Chicago.